Law, Literature and Society

CSANA Yearbook 7

EDITORIAL STATEMENT

A Celtic studies periodical for the new millennium, the *Celtic Studies Association of North America Yearbook* features articles on a wide range of subjects of interest to Celticists and scholars in other fields. *CSANAY* seeks to foster interdisciplinary and ground-breaking approaches to Celtic studies, and to complement, rather than duplicate, the missions of other journals of Celtic studies. Each issue of *CSANAY* features its own theme, and the themes of future issues (as well as calls for papers pertaining to those themes) are announced in the *CSANA newsletter*. For information about subscribing to the *CSANA newsletter* and joining CSANA, which is open to all with a scholarly interest in Celtic studies and offers *CSANA* at a reduced price to its members, please visit the website at: http://www.csub.edu/~macquarrie/csana/ or contact the Secretary-Treasurer, Prof. Elissa R. Henken, Department of English, Park Hall, University of Georgia, Athens, GA 30602, USA <ehenken@arches.uga.edu>.

Contributors to *CSANAY* are normally members of CSANA, but the Editor welcomes all scholarly submissions, especially those from younger scholars. Each submitted article is read and evaluated by two experts in the relevant field, whose reports guide the Editor and the Editorial Board in their final decision. Questions concerning *CSANAY* should be addressed to the editor, Prof. Joseph F. Eska, Department of English, Virginia Polytechnic Institute & State University, Blacksburg, VA 24061, USA <eska@vt.edu>.

Law, Literature and Society

CSANA Yearbook 7

Joseph F. Eska
EDITOR

FOUR COURTS PRESS

Typeset in 11pt on 13pt Bembo by
Carrigboy Typesetting Services for
FOUR COURTS PRESS LTD
7 Malpas Street, Dublin 8, Ireland
e-mail: info@fourcourtspress.ie
and in North America for
FOUR COURTS PRESS
c/o ISBS, 920 N.E. 58th Avenue, Suite 300, Portland, OR 97213.

A catalogue record for this title is available
from the British Library.

ISSN 1649–0096
ISBN 978–1–84682–099–1

Printed in England
by CPI Antony Rowe, Chippenham, Wilts.

Contents

Introduction

JOSEPH F. ESKA

Over the last quarter-century, the intimate relationship of the study of law and literature has become increasingly clear in the field of medieval Celtic studies. Knowledge of the legal tracts can help us to understand the events that occur in literary texts,[1] passages in literary texts can help us fill out gaps in the law tracts, and both subjects can help us to contextualize what we know of historical events and social institutions. The relationship has been well stated by Robin Chapman Stacey on a number of occasions, e.g.:

> The boundary between law and literature has never been particularly hard and fast … [L]iterature has long been for medievalists a fruitful source of examples of 'custom in action' – a way in which to contextualize and enlarge upon the schematic rigidity of the principles articulated in the lawbooks of the period.[2]

> One of the most striking trends in contemporary legal scholarship has been the increasing tendency of specialists to treat law and literature as related, or even inter-related, genres … Medievalists also have taken up such questions, in some cases drawing on literature to enlarge their understanding of practices glimpsed only dimly in the legal documents, in others using law to resolve cruxes of plot or motivation. To date, their studies have been predicated on the idea that law and literature share a common cultural background and can therefore be used to elucidate or expand upon one another. This is undoubtedly right; in medieval Ireland and Wales, close ties existed between members of the legal and literary professions …
>
> … [I]n these two cultures law was, in a very real sense, a branch of literature.[3]

1 For an example, see Tomás Ó Cathasaigh, *Táin bó Cúailnge and early Irish law* (Baile Átha Cliath: Dámh an Léinn Cheiltigh, An Coláiste Ollscoile, 2005). 2 Robin Chapman Stacey, 'Divorce, medieval Welsh style', *Speculum* 77 (2002), 1107–27 at 1107. 3 Robin Chapman Stacey, 'Law and

CSANA Yearbook 7: Four Courts Press, Dublin; ISSN 1649–0096; ISBN 978–1–84682–099–1

The majority of papers in this volume of the *CSANA Yearbook* seek to cast light on this close relationship between law and literature, and to offer some examples of what each can do for the study of the other, as well as for history and society.

Paul Russell's opening paper examines the literary narratives that are contained within *Sanas Cormaic* to test whether there is any linkage between them. That there does, indeed, seem to be promise in this approach may cast light on the interests of the compilers of this interesting text which contains significant legal information. Sara Elin Roberts, on the other hand, studies the legal triads of medieval Wales which focus on the law of women. She demonstrates that the continuing composition of legal material in this literary form provided a venue for the development of medieval Welsh law.

Two articles focus on the figure of Derbforgaill, the twelfth-century woman who has been seen by most Irish writers through the centuries as bearing much of the responsibility for the Norman invasion of Ireland. Lahney Preston-Matto shows, however, that a knowledge of Irish marriage law and the politics of the time reveals that she took no wrong action, which explains why contemporaneous Irish annals pass little judgment upon her, while Anglo-Norman sources, unaware of these facts, of course, do. Karen Eileen Overbey carries on to show, in the context of Derbforgaill's role as patron for the construction of the Nun's Church, that, as the figure held to be responsible for the Norman invasion, she has largely been removed from history and become, instead, mythologized as a marker of the transition from Gaelic to Norman Ireland.

Michael Meckler's article looks at the law of kinship in relation to the assassination of Diarmait mac Cerbaill in 565, and argues that the use of the term *occisio* rather than *iugulatio* may reflect an understanding of the distinction in Irish law between intentional homicides that could be classified as forgivable slayings and those that could not.

Finally, Timothy P. Bridgman examines the question of 'What's in a name?' He addresses the question of whether the ethnic designations of the Celts used by early Greek writers, indeed, are potentially Celtic self-designations or merely descriptors, and where these 'names' may have come from.

literature in medieval Ireland and Wales' in Helen Fulton (ed.), *Medieval Celtic literature and society* (Dublin: Four Courts Press, 2005), pp 65–82 at 65.

Poets, Power and Possessions in Medieval Ireland: Some Stories from *Sanas Cormaic*

PAUL RUSSELL

Scattered through the early Irish encyclopaedic glossary, known as *Sanas Cormaic* (henceforth *SC*), among the many shorter entries explaining and etymologizing Irish words, some longer entries are preserved which contain brief but complete narratives.[1] In the entry on *gaire* (Y 698, *SC* G29), the un-named wife of Caíer, king of Connacht, falls in love with Néide, Caíer's nephew and adopted son, and persuades him to make a satire against Caíer so that Néide might take over the kingship and her in his place.[2] She

1 For general discussion of *SC* and the early Irish glossary tradition, see Paul Russell, 'The sounds of a silence: the growth of Cormac's Glossary', *Cambridge Medieval Celtic Studies*, 15 (1988), 1–30, and W. Mahon, 'Contributions to the study of early Irish lexicography' (PhD, Harvard University, 1987); refinements and developments can be found in Paul Russell, '*Dúil Dromma Cetta* and Cormac's Glossary', *Études Celtiques* 32 (1996), 147–74, and 'Laws, glossaries and legal glossaries', *Zeitschrift für Celtische Philologie* 51 (1998), 85–115. Translations of all the stories discussed in this paper are in the Appendix (pp 33–43). References to entries in *SC* are given in a double format: first, its number in Y (for abbreviations to the different glossary versions, see the Abbreviations below, pp 43–4), and secondly, its number in our new forthcoming edition of *SC* where items are numbered within each letter-block.

A version of this paper was presented at the Centre for Medieval and Renaissance Studies at UCLA in January 2007; I am grateful for their kind invitation and support, and in particular to Joseph Nagy for his generous hospitality and to Karen Burgess for all her kind help. The research for this paper arose out of the Early Irish Glossaries Project, funded by the UK Arts and Humanities Research Council, in the Dept of Anglo-Saxon, Norse and Celtic, University of Cambridge, a three-year project (1 July 2006–30 June 2009) involving Dr Paul Russell, Dr Sharon Arbuthnot and Dr Padraic Moran. Its aim is to produce modern editions of the three main early Irish glossaries: *Sanas Cormaic, Dúil Dromma Cetta* and O'Mulconry's Glossary. Already on-line is the *Early Irish Glossaries Database*, with Padraic Moran (Cambridge, 2006) http://www.asnc.cam.ac.uk/irishglossaries/ (also accessible via the ASNC website) where it is possible to search the glossary headwords and to create concordances. I am grateful to Sharon Arbuthnot, Padraic Moran and Charlene Eska for reading and commenting on earlier drafts of this paper, although not necessarily agreeing with what follows. **2** For more specific discussion of the *Gaire* entry in *SC* in the context of satire, see Howard Meroney, 'Studies in early Irish satire', *Journal of Celtic Studies* 1 (1949–50), 199–226 at 212–26. The crucial satirical verse at the core of the narrative has been discussed on numerous occasions; see, for example, Liam Breatnach (ed.), *Uraicecht na ríar* (Dublin: DIAS, 1987), p. 115 (with notes on p. 137).

CSANA Yearbook 7: Four Courts Press, Dublin; ISSN 1649–0096; ISBN 978–1–84682–099–1

presents Néide with a carefully devised plan by which Néide can extract a refusal from Caíer and consequently utter a disfiguring satire against him. The request Néide makes, and which inevitably has to be refused, is for a knife Caíer was given in the lands of Alba which he is prohibited by a *géis* from giving away. The scheme goes to plan but with the expected disastrous outcome for all the protagonists.[3]

We may contrast this episode with the narrative preserved elsewhere in *SC* in the entry on *Mug Éime* (Y 883, *SC* M33), where once again a knife is central to the narrative.[4] Coirpre Músc is visiting friends in Britain and takes a liking to a lap-dog – a species not to be found in Ireland at this time.[5] Coirpre asks his friend for the lap-dog, but is refused; it appears that the Britons have proclaimed a monopoly over them and declared that they should not be exported whatever the inducement. Perhaps on account of friendship or kinship, or mindful of the catastrophic consequences, Coirpre does not resort to satire against his friend even though he clearly moves in royal circles. Instead, he cleverly exploits the laws of the Britons themselves to obtain what he wants. He leaves a finely-wrought knife lying around overnight with its handle (*éim*) liberally smeared with bacon – and beef-fat. Predictably, the lap-dog finds this irresistable and spends the night gnawing at it. The hilt of the knife is thus irreparably damaged. As a result, Coirpre is able to invoke *Cáin Bretan* 'a law of the Britons', 'every animal for its crime', and so obtains the lap-dog as recompense for his damaged knife.[6] Rather than go down the inevitably disastrous path of satire as Néide and his stepmother did, Coirpre exploits the legal system of the Britons to get what he wanted. While the stakes in the latter case are lower – it is not a case of dynastic politics, but rather a dispute between friends about the ownership of a lap-dog – the difference in approach is striking and interesting and

3 See Meroney, 'Studies in early Irish satire', 212–26; Robin Chapman Stacey, *Dark speech: the performance of law in early Ireland* (Philadephia: University of Pennsylvania Press, 2007), pp 109–10. It is usually assumed that Néide is killed at the end, but it is arguable that he may simply have been sufficiently disfigured that he would have been barred from the kingship, an outcome which to us at least might seem more satisfactory. For satire in early Ireland, see Liam Breatnach, 'An aoir sa ré luath', *Léachtaí Cholm Cille* 18 (1988), 11–19; Liam Breatnach, 'On satire and the poet's circuit' in C.G. Ó Háinle and D.E. Meek (eds), *Unity in diversity: studies in Irish and Scottish Gaelic language, literature and history* (Dublin: School of Irish, Trinity College, Dublin, 2004), 25–35, Liam Breatnach; 'Satire and praise and the early Irish poet', *Ériu* 56 (2006), 63–84. **4** This entry has received less attention generally; for discussion of the British word quoted, see Paul Russell, 'Brittonic words in early Irish glossaries' in J.F. Eska, R.G. Gruffydd and N. Jacobs (eds), *Hispano-Gallo-Brittonica: essays in honour of Professor D. Ellis Evans on the occasion of his sixty-fifth birthday* (Cardiff: University of Wales Press, 1995), pp 166–82 at pp 168 and 179; for the Cornish aspect, see Charles Thomas, *And shall these mute stones speak?* (Cardiff: University of Wales Press, 1994), pp 44–6. **5** On lap-dogs in Ireland, see Fergus Kelly, *Early Irish farming* (Dublin: Dublin Institute for Advanced Studies, 1997), pp 120–1. **6** For discussion of *Cáin Bretan*, see below, pp 24–6.

further aspects are discussed below. This lap-dog was pregnant and became the ancestor of all the lap-dogs in Ireland; the narrative continues as a parody of an origin legend to show how the pups were distributed throughout Ireland and became the ancestors of all the lap-dogs in Ireland. We may however note the cautionary *ut Scoti perhibent* 'so the Irish say' added by the narrator to the end of this part of the story. That all of this in the view of the narrator happened at some distant point in the past is also suggested by the fact that, many years after the dog died, divination was required to identify the skull of the dog as all memory of it had faded.

The poet called upon to make a divination in this case was Máen mac Etna after the skull had been discovered by Conlae mac Taidc meic Chéin meic Ailella Óloimm. It is worth pointing out that Conlae seems to have been the brother of Cormac mac Taidc who in the entry on the origin of the name of the Gaileng (Y 685, *SC* G16) was responsible for feeding badger-meat, his name-taboo food, to Tadc, his father.[7] As a result he became known as Cormac Gaileng, literally etymologised as 'spear-disgrace'. Yet another lap-dog figures in *SC* at the end of the entry on Coire Brecáin (Y 323, *SC* C122) when Lugaid Dall Éces announces the death of Brecán in the whirlpool on the basis of divination of a tiny skull found on the beach at Inber Bec which he proclaims to be the skull of Brecán's lap-dog. Another lap-dog did therefore in fact reach Ireland – but not alive and perhaps only its skull. We are also reminded here of Finn's identification of Lomna from his headless corpse in *Orc Tréith*. Similarly, the narrative on Brecán who perished in the eponymous Coire Brecáin recalls another entry in *SC* on Manannán mac Lir (Y 896, *SC* M46), another famous merchant of the Irish Sea area. The latter entry provides an explanation of his name deriving it from the name of the Isle of Man – the location of the longest entry in *SC*, *Prull* (Y 1059, *SC* P19), in which Senchán Torpéist is upstaged by the Spirit of Poetry but succeeds in locating the female poet, the daughter of úa Dulsaine.

The longer, more narrative, entries discussed here include *Coire Brecáin* (Y 323 = *SC* C122), *Gaileng* (Y 685, *SC* G16), *Greth* (Y 690 = *SC* G21), *Gaire* (Y 698 = *SC* G29), *Imbas for·osnai* (Y 756 = *SC* I24), *Lethech* (Y 825 = *SC* L33), *Mug Éime* (Y 883 = *SC* M33), *Orc tréith* (Y 1018 = *SC* O21) and *Prull* (Y 1059 = *SC* P19); working translations are provided in the Appendix (pp 3–43).[8] These entries are usually located at the end or towards the end of

7 For discussion of this entry, see Alan Mac an Bhaird, 'Varia II: Tadhg mac Céin and the badgers', *Ériu* 31 (1980), 150–5. 8 Many of these entries have been edited and/or translated, either wholly or partially, elsewhere: for *Coire Brecáin*, see Richard Sharpe (trans.), *Adomnán of Iona, Life of St Columba* (London: Penguin, 1995), pp 264–5; for *Gaileng*, Mac an Bhaird, 'Varia II: Tadhg mac Céin and the badgers'; for *Greth*, cf. Patrick Ford, 'The blind, the dumb, and the ugly: aspects of poets and their craft in early Ireland and Wales', *Cambridge Medieval Celtic Studies* 19 (1990), 27–40 at 28–30, and also John T. Koch and John Carey, *The Celtic heroic age: literary sources for ancient Celtic Europe and*

letter blocks in the short version of *SC*, preserved in La, M and B, and they are also preserved in the longer versions of the glossary, Y, H^{1a} and H^{1b}, though with extra entries added after them at the end of each letter block. All the entries in *SC*, and indeed other medieval Irish glossaries, are intended to explain the headword of the entry. That explanation can involve greater or lesser degrees of complexity and take a number of forms: they can simply provide a meaning, as in a modern dictionary entry, often in the form *A .i. B*, e.g. Y 207, *SC* C4 *cobthach .i. búadach* 'i.e. victorious'. Others provide etymological analysis, where the word is sub-divided into to smaller, meaningful elements, e.g. Y 233, *SC* C29 *conair .i. cen fér, cen ar* '*conair* (path), [*cen* 'without' + *fér* 'grass', or *cen* 'without' + *ar* 'ploughing'] i.e. without grass, without ploughing'. In some instances, the analysis is followed by explanation, Y 244, *SC* C40 *capull .i. cap carr 7 peall ech. Do chapall carr 7 eiri is nomen* '*capull* (horse), i.e. *cap* "wagon" and *peall* "horse". It is the name for a cart-horse and a pack-horse'. Other languages can be called on to provide the etymology, frequently Latin (but also on occasions Greek or Hebrew), e.g. Y 16, *SC* A19 *arged ab argento*, Y 22, *SC* A23 *adamra .i. ab admiratione*, and sometimes with a larger explanatory framework, such as *ab eo quod est* (= Irish *dindí as, óndí as*), e.g. Y 64, *SC* A65 *áiminn ab eo quod est amoenum .i. áibind*, Y 13, *SC* A14 *ar ab eo quod est aro .i. airim*, Y 11, *SC* A12 *aicher ab eo quod est acer .i. lainn nó tind nó trén* (typically in such cases the Irish translation of the Latin is only preserved in manuscripts of the Y-group, the longer version). If a degree of 'bridging', or formal manipulation of the headword, is required to make the etymology fit, *quasi* can be used to mark the 'bridge' form, e.g. Y 643, *SC* F69 *fúal quasi fuil ar a dath, vel quasi búal .i. uisce* '*fúal* (urine) as if *fuil* (blood) on account of its colour, or as if *búal* (water), i.e. water',

early Ireland and Wales (4th ed., Aberystwyth: Celtic Studies Publications, 2003), pp 65–6, in both of which the Book of Leinster version of the story is translated; for *Gaire*, see Whitley Stokes, *Three Irish glossaries* (London: Williams & Norgate, 1862 (repr. Felinfach: Llanerch, 2000)), pp xxxvi–xl; for a translation of the satire itself, see Meroney, 'Studies in early Irish satire', 215; for *Imbas for·osnai*, Joseph Nagy, *The Wisdom of the outlaw: the boyhood deeds of Finn in Gaelic narrative tradition* (Berkeley: University of California Press, 1985), pp 25–6; Patrick Ford, *The Celtic poets: songs and tales from early Ireland and Wales* (Belmont, MA: Ford & Bailie, 1999), p. 47; Paul Russell, 'Notes on words in early Irish glossaries', *Études celtiques* 31 (1995), 198–204 at 198–200; for *Orc tréith*, see Thomas Clancy, 'Fools and adultery in some early Irish texts', *Ériu* 44 (1993), 105–24 at 110–11; Ford, *Celtic poets*, pp 53–4; for *Prull*, see Rudolf Thurneysen, 'Zu Cormacs Glossar' in *Festschrift Ernst Windisch zum siebzigsten Geburtstag am 4. September 1914 dargebracht von Freunden und Schülern* (Leipzig: Harassowitz, 1914), pp 8–37, repr. in R. Thurneysen, *Gesammelte Schriften*, Band II, ed. P. de Bernardo-Stempel and R. Ködderitzsch (Tübingen: Niemeyer, 1991), pp 188–217) (in German); Ford, *Celtic poets*, pp 39–42; Ford, 'The blind, the dumb, and the ugly', 30–4; Anne Dooley, 'Early Irish literature and contemporary scholarly disciplines' in R. Wall (ed.), *Modern and medieval Ireland* (Totowa, NJ: Barnes & Noble, 1988), pp 60–74 at p. 68–71; Máirín Ní Dhonnchadha, 'The *Prull* narrative in *Sanais Cormaic*' in J. Carey, M. Herbert and K. Murray (eds), *Cín Chille Cúile: texts, saints and places. Essays in honour of Pádraig Ó Riain* (Aberystwyth: Celtic Studies Publications, 2004), pp 163–77 at pp 164–7.

Y 742, *SC* I10 *imbliu quasi umbliu ab umbilico* ...[9] Matters can become more complicated, such as when multiple etymologies are provided; see, for example, Y 344, *SC* C143 *cúal .i. óna cuillib bís inte as·berur, vel quasi gúal .i. ón gúaland, ar is fuirre bis a truma, vel quasi caol a calon latine* (recte *graece*) '*cúal* (bundle of sticks), i.e. it is so called from the sticks which are in it, or as if *gúal*, i.e. from the shoulder upon which its burden is, or as if *caol* from Greek *kâlon*', where three possible explanations are provided.[10] Another typical mode of presentation is to provide a quotation exemplifying the use of the word:[11]

> Y 26, SC A27 Art tréde for·dingair .i. art .i. úasal, unde dicitur 'art fine'. Art .i. día, unde dicitur Eochaid Find Fúath n-Airt .i. fúath déa fair ara chaíme. Item Cú Chulainn *post mortem dicere perhibetur* 'Do·memaid art úasal', .i. día úasal. Art dono cloch nó leac ligi, *cuius diminutivum* arténe, .i. cloichéne, .i. ainm disbecad, unde Gúaire Aidne dixit:
>
> Do·celat
> mór n-amrae ind airténi
> bíte for lige Marcáin
> maic Aeda maic Maircéni.
>
> *Art* means three things: art, i.e. high, thus *art fine* 'head of the kin'. Art, i.e. god, thus Eochaid Find Fúath n-Airt, i.e. the likeness of a god upon him on account of his beauty. Similarly, Cú Chulainn is *claimed to have said after his death*, 'a high *art* has burst forth', i.e. a high god. *Art*, then, is a stone or a grave stone, *the diminutive of which is arténe*, i.e. a little stone, i.e. a diminutive noun, thus Gúaire Aidne said:
>
> They conceal
> a great wonder, the little stones
> which are upon the grave of Marcán,
> mac Aedha meic Maircéni.

In this case, in which three different interpretations of *art* have been brought together, the second and third explanations are exemplified by quotations:

9 Paul Russell, '*Quasi*: bridging the etymological gap in early Irish glossaries' in B. Smelik, R. Hofman et al. (eds), *A companion in linguistics: a festschrift for Anders Ahlqvist on the occasion of his sixtieth birthday* (Nijmegen: Draak, 2005), pp 49–62. **10** For further discussion of entries containing Greek, see Paul Russell, '*Graece* ... *Latine*: Graeco-Latin glossaries in early medieval Ireland', *Peritia* 14 (2000), 406–20. **11** For discussion of this entry and of the process of creating double, triple and quadruple entries from entries which are attested separately in other glossaries, see Russell, 'Sounds of a silence', 29–30.

the former can be traced to *Brislech Mór Maige Muirthemni* (L 122^b48 = l. 14191), and the latter (not found elsewhere) does not in fact contain the headword, but rather its diminutive form, *arténe*.

However long and narrative an entry might be, structurally it fits into one of the above types. For example, *gaire* is the first word and a key word in the satirical verse uttered by Néide against Caíer and in the first lines of the entry is etymologised as *.i. gair seclae, .i. gair ré, .i. ré gair* 'i.e. short life, [< *gair* 'short' + *ré* 'period of time'], i.e. short time'; this then leads seamlessly into the narrative in which the satire itself is embedded. Entries such as *Mug Éime*, *Gaileng*, *Greth* etc. fit more into the mould of explanation of names of people or peoples, best represented by the collections of *Cóir Anmann*, while *Coire Brecáin* is closer to the place-name explanations found in the *Dindṡenchas*.[12] Such entries vary in their approach too; some simply give a lengthy explanation of why someone or somewhere is so called (*Coire Brecáin*, *Mug Éime*, *Greth*), while others provide explanation through etymology (*Gaileng*). On the other hand, an entry such as *Lethech* approaches its core narrative more obliquely: it is given two meanings, first, a flatfish, and secondly a word for a trough in which bread-dough is kneaded. It emerges eventually in the following narrative that *lethech* 'kneading-trough' is key to understanding the story, precisely because the apprentice-poet does not understand what the word means. Similarly, in *Prull* the adverb *prull* 'greatly' figures in the key quatrain that Senchán Torpéist fails to complete. It is typical of the structure of these stories that the key moment which usually contains the headword of the passage is brought to the front of the story and then the rest of the narrative is structured to bring the audience back to that point. *Mug Éime* presents all the ingredients first, the first lap-dog, Coirpre Músc, relationships between Ireland and Britain, before we get to find out how they come together. *Coire Brecáin* has two elements to the headword, the whirlpool and Brecán, and we are introduced to each in turn, starting with the whirlpool, before they are brought together in the final section; it ends chiastically with Brecán and the *coire* appearing in that order in the final sentence, almost as if the whirpool was surrounding Brecán. The effect, then, is often that the headword can function as a *dúnad* in the narrative; the story

12 For *Cóir Anmann*, see now the new editions of the different versions by Sharon Arbuthnot (ed.), *Cóir Anmann: a late Middle-Irish treatise on personal names* (Part 1), Irish Texts Society, 59 (Dublin: Irish Texts Society, 2005), (Part 2), Irish Texts Society, 60 (Dublin: Irish Texts Society, 2007); for the *Dindṡenchas*, see Whitley Stokes, 'The Bodleian Dindshenchas', *Folklore* 3 (1892), 467–516; Whitley Stokes, 'The Edinburgh Dindshenchas', *Folklore* 4 (1893), 471–97; Whitley Stokes, 'The prose tales in the Rennes Dindshenchas', *Revue celtique* 15 (1894), 222–336 and 418–84, 16 (1895), 31–83, 135–67 and 269–312; E.J. Gwynn, *Poems from the Dindshenchas*, Todd Lecture Series, 7 (Dublin: Hodges & Figgis, 1900); Whitley Stokes, *The metrical Dindshenchas*, 5 vols, Todd Lecture Series, 8–12 (Dublin: Hodges & Figgis, 1903–35).

begins and ends with the same word. Put another way, in some of these entries, then, the narrative functions like a giant quotation.

The criss-crossing references between these narrative entries, some of which have been randomly sketched above, would by themselves encourage us to think it worthwhile to explore these longer entries as a group. There are further reasons to think in such terms. It is clear from previous work on these glossaries that they are works of compilation.[13] While at some relatively remote stage in their formation glosses might have been culled from texts and put into textual order and then alphabeticized, the immediately preceding phases of glossary-creation seems to have involved gathering in glossary material from wherever it might be found. This is most easily seen in the short glossary, labelled H², preserved in Dublin, Trinity College, 1337 (H.3.18), pp 76–83 (= *CIH* ii 622.13–633.3), where the manuscript still shows traces of layers of copying with small blocks of entries added at the bottom of columns of text or inserted in a space at the end of a letter block; a fair copy of that manuscript, if it was ever made, would have concealed that process of compilation. If we accept the principle of compilation from multiple sources as the main way in which these glossaries were constructed, it is even more remarkable that these narrative entries have such criss-crossing connections unless they derive from the same source or were gathered with a particular purpose in mind. There are further structural reasons for pursuing this line of thought. Within each letter-block, glossaries such as *SC* are typically ordered by first letter only, what is called α-ordering (as opposed to modern alphabetical ordering which orders words by the letter-order all the way through the word). The fact that within letter blocks entries are ordered by first letter only without further alphabeticization allows us to see some of the layers of compilation with a letter block. In other words, new material being added to a glossary would simply be placed at the end of a letter block and not interspersed within a complex alphabetic listing. I have argued this in detail for some of the legal material found in *SC*;[14] it seems likely that clusters of entries based on the same legal text were added to different letter blocks of the glossary at the same time, and that material from different legal texts were added at different times. The argument is based on the assumption that, if material deriving from the same text is found in a number of letter blocks and it occurs proportionally at about the same point in the letter block, then it is likely that it arrived in the glossary at the same time. The proposition has since been strengthened by Liam Breatnach's work on the sources feeding into O'Davoren's Glossary, a glossary of legal words;[15] he has shown that blocks of quotations deriving

13 See Russell, '*Dúil Dromma Cetta* and Cormac's Glossary'; Russell, 'Laws, glossaries and legal glossaries'. **14** Russell, 'Laws, glossaries and legal glossaries', pp 111–13. **15** Liam Breatnach, *A*

from the same source cluster in groups within a letter block. It is reasonable to suppose that a few entries may have been moved around subsequently for stylistic effect, and particularly moved to the front of a letter block, e.g. *Adam*, *bendacht*, *Corbmac*, *Iesu*, *Modebroth* (Patrick's British oath), *nia* (containing a prophecy about the coming of Christ) etc., or to create blocks of two or three explanations of synonyms (a feature characteristic of *SC*).[16] Even so, the majority of entries seem to have remained where they were put. Now, if the above proposition is accepted in general terms, then the fact that a number of letter blocks in the short versions of *SC* end with a long narrative entry begins to look significant. However, there is a number of ways in which it could be significant: it is possible that they derive from the same source, but alternatively the end of a letter block may have been as important a place for relocating an entry as the beginning of a letter block, and it is conceivable that entries were moved to that position. On the other hand, not all letter blocks end in a narrative entry or indeed contain narrative entries at all, and conversely some letter blocks contain more than one narrative entry (e.g. *G* with *Greth*, *Gaileng* and *Gaire*). There may, therefore, have been other reasons for selecting and incorporating these particular entries into *SC* and indeed for moving them to significant places within the letter block. Further evidence for thinking of these entries as a group is suggested by Proinsias Mac Cana's plausible proposal that the ending of the *Coire Brecáin* entry, where a lap-dog skull is found, was modelled on the ending of *Mug Éime* through a misunderstanding of *oircne* as 'lap-dog' rather than as 'destruction';[17] if so, at some point in the compiling of *SC* at least one compiler was thinking that there were links between these narrative entries.

A number of these long entries have been discussed in detail in their own terms as individual narratives, some indeed on several occasions: Patrick Ford (on *Greth* and *Prull*), Thomas Clancy (on *Orc tréith*), Máirín Ní Dhonnchadha (on *Prull*) and Alan Mac an Bhaird (on *Gaileng*) have all made important contributions to our understanding of these entries as individual narratives.[18] One feature of these studies is they often draw on related versions of the narratives which occur elsewhere; for example, in his discussion of *Greth*, Ford also makes use of the longer and more detailed version preserved in the Book of Leinster;[19] similarly Mac an Bhaird considers several versions of the Gaileng story;[20] Mac Cana examines the relationship

companion to the Corpus iuris Hibernici (Dublin: DIAS, 2005), pp 100–59, esp. pp 103–4. **16** For discussion of the former, see Russell, 'Laws, glossaries and legal glossaries', 12; for the latter, see the example of *art* quoted above (p. 13) or the beginning of *Lethech*. **17** Proinsias Mac Cana, *The learned tales of medieval Ireland* (Dublin: DIAS, 1980), p. 150. **18** Ford, 'The blind, the dumb, and the ugly'; Clancy, 'Fools and adultery'; Ní Dhonnchadha, 'The *Prull* narrative'; Mac an Bhaird, 'Varia II: Tadhg mac Céin and the badgers'. **19** Ford, 'The blind, the dumb, and the ugly', 25–30. **20** Mac an Bhaird, 'Varia II: Tadhg mac Céin and the badgers'; he seems not to have been aware of the

between the Coire Brecáin entry and the versions preserved in the prose and verse *Dindšenchas*;[21] and Dillon has edited another version of the Finn and Lomna narrative (found as part of *Orc tréith* (Y 1018, *SC* O21)) as one of the legal stories preserved in Dublin, Trinity College, 1336 (H.3.17).[22] While that approach is perfectly legitimate in considering the broader literary context of these narratives (and indeed there are occasions when reference will be made to the other versions), this study is less concerned with external links and we are more interested in considering these entries as a group or at least as an interrelated cluster of entries within *SC*. This is not to imply that other scholars have not used these stories for comparative purposes; both Ford and Ní Dhonnchadha, for example, have profitably set *Greth* and *Prull* side by side.[23] It is suggested here, however, that consideration of the themes contained in these narratives may allow us to gain a clearer understanding of the original and principal concerns of the compilers of the short version of *SC*, especially if those concerns can also be detected elsewhere in the glossary as well. The central part of this paper therefore considers a number of the themes which can be seen to link these narrative entries. It does not attempt to provide complete readings of each story nor even to tell the stories, but rather to explore what they may have in common.

It is worth pointing out that, when we refer to these narratives in *SC*, not all versions of the glossary contain exactly the same form of the narratives. Generally, following the principles of the Early Irish Glossary Project to provide editions of the fullest versions of the glossaries, the version translated in the Appendix is usually that found in the Y group of *SC*. However, it is worth noting out that, in B and M, *Greth* and *Gaire* contain only the quotation of Amairgen's words and the satirical verse, respectively, and that it is only in Y is there any narrative. In the Y group version of *Coire Brecáin*, there are two accounts of Brecán, but in B only one of those acounts is found and in the M version (La is lacking at that point) the other is preserved; it would appear then that the Y group preserves a composite version. In *Prull*, matters are yet more complicated: while B has a longer version of the nasty description of the youth, B, La and M preserve a shorter version of the beautiful description of him; the translation in the Appendix follows Y, but prints the extra description from B underneath. In other words, when it comes to discussing the glossary context of these longer entries, it has to be borne in mind that usually any general comment about these entries as a group can strictly only apply to the Y group, as there is no guarantee that the other versions have the same versions.

mainly Latin version of the story preserved in the genealogies; see M.A. O'Brien (ed.), *Corpus genealogiarum Hiberniae*, vol. 1 (Dublin: DIAS, 1962), pp 246–7. **21** Mac Cana, *The learned tales*, pp 146–50. **22** Myles Dillon, 'Stories from the law tracts', *Ériu* 11 (1932), 42–65 at 58–61. **23** Ford,

A striking feature of these stories is their interest in the activities of poets – from the first stirrings of poetic inspiration through the process of education, of becoming a poet, to poets in all their pomp with a full panoply of followers. We often see the great poets, such as Athairne in *Greth* or Cruitíne in *Lethech*, refracted through the behaviour of their retainers or students. Greth, the servant (or perhaps student) of Athairne, is sent to Ecet Salach, the smith, to ask for a loan.[24] He sees sitting by the fire a tiny seven-year-old who proceeds to utter an alliterating run based on Greth's name: '*In·ith Greth gruth, .i. fonaithe, gríanmaine, gránmune, gais crema, cúe, .i. cnú, uinn, ubla grethi, grith?*' which, stripped of its glosses, seems to mean something like 'Does Greth eat curds, blackberries (?), sloes (?), sprigs of wild garlic, pine-nuts, sour (?) apples, curds?'.[25] It is clear that Greth has no idea what this means and reports back to Athairne who, realizing that the boy is his future rival, Amairgen, resolves to cut his life short. The attempt on Amairgen's life fails and Athairne is bound into teaching him all he knows. Thus the first encounter between Athairne and Amairgen is mediated through Greth, the unknowing *gilla*, and involves a failure of understanding even as Greth's very own name acts as the bridge for the alliterative utterance. Within these narratives the great poets are far too grand to carry out these menial activities for themselves, but their presence in the margins of the opening scenes of these narratives is always felt. The structure of the *Lethech* episode is strikingly similar to the *Greth* story. A go-between, this time an over-confident student, is sent to a poet's house with his teacher, Cruitíne, lurking in the undergrowth outside and on the margins of the story. Similarly, the story turns on the student's inability to understand the high-flown language of Cruitíne's colleague just as Greth failed to understand Amairgen.

The opening sentence of *Greth* presents all the characters in a list, rather like a cast of a play: *Greth ainm gilla Athairne,* cui *Amargein mac Ecet Salach goband ó Búais* dixit 'Greth, the name of the Athairne's servant, to whom Amairgen, the son of Ecet Salach, a smith from Bush, spoke'. That the sparse grammatical frame of this opening sentence is in Latin, … *cui* … *dixit*, should perhaps give us pause for thought. While a Latinate grammatical or syntactical framework is extremely common in the early Irish glossaries generally,

'The blind, the dumb, and the ugly'; Ní Dhonnchadha, 'The *Prull* narrative'. **24** For a discussion of the different possible sense of *gilla*, see below, p. 32. The reason for Greth going to Ecet Salach is less than clear either in the *SC* version or the Book of Leinster version; in *SC*, Greth comes *do chuinchid íasachto* 'to seek a loan' (of what is not made clear), while in the Book of Leinster it is *do chor béla i teinid* 'to put an axe in a fire', presumably to have an axe repaired by the smith, an implement which becomes significant in that narrative as the attempted murder weapon. It may be that the link is that in *SC* he was coming to borrow an axe. **25** The translation is provisional, but we may note the binding alliteration of initial consonants linking the first element of a bipartite phrase to the last element (or only element) of the preceding phrase, e.g. (ignoring glosses) ***g**ránmune, **g**ais crema, **c**úe **u**inn, **u**bla **g**rethi, **g**rith.*

the use of Latin in these longer entries usually occurs at significant moments. This is the only one of the long entries to begin with a Latinate structure and, while it is difficult to be clear precisely why Latin was chosen here, it does have the striking effect of allowing the names of Athairne and Amairgen to be juxtaposed. Two further examples may make the point. In *Prull*, when Senchán Torpéist reaches Man after a rather over-full boat-trip from Ireland, he and his retinue see an old woman on the rocks reaping seaweed. At that point, the direct narrative pauses and the narrator fills in the back-narrative for his audience. He presents a quatrain and identifies the woman as the female poet, the daughter of úa Dulsaine. The start of the digression is marked with *ut poeta dixit* and the end by *et rel.*; in other words, we are given only as much of the back-story to make sense of what is to come. Significantly, the digression is framed in Latin. Again, at the end of the narrative in which Senchán has been upstaged by the scabby lad who can cap the verses more quickly and effectively than Senchán himself, the retinue of poets return to Ireland in triumph with the female-poet, now bathed and properly dressed, only to be met by the *gilla remeperthae* 'the afore-mentioned lad' now transformed into a 'radiant, kingly youth'. Just as we have been invited to compare the before and after of the transformed female-poet, so we should set side-by-side the gruesome and the glowing description of the lad. The phrase, *gilla remeperthae*, is noteworthy: all its other attestations listed in *DIL* are in a clearly Latinate context, mainly used for cross-referencing between glosses, and it is a transparent calque on *supradictus* or the like. As such, we should therefore be prepared for the Latin which follows the brilliant description and ends the story: *et nusquam aparuit ex illo tempore. Dubium itaque non est quod ille Poematis erat spiritus*. The marked nature of the Latin coda tells us what we may have suspected – that this is a comment by the narrator. In *Prull*, therefore, it looks as if one use of Latin is to indicate narratorial comment. Similarly, as we have seen, in *Mug Éime*, the clause *ut Scotti perhibent* also marks a rather sceptical observation by the narrator, one which also carries with it a sense that the narrator wishes to distance himself from the observation: that is, 'others might think this, but I am not so sure …'. A similar distancing technique occurs in the entry on Manannán mac Lir where, after the admiring comments about the excellence of his seamanship, it is remarked with a note of scepticism *inde Scoti et Britones eum deum uocauerunt maris, et inde filium maris esse dixerunt* .i. mac lir 'As a result the Irish and the Britons called him a god of the sea, and so said that he was the son of the sea, i.e. *mac lir*'. On the other hand, it is striking that in *Coire Brecáin* Latin is used to frame the act of divination which confirms the death of Brecán, while the arguably parallel act of divination in *Mug Éime* is framed in the vernacular.[26] An even more telling use of Latin perhaps occurs

26 For the possible connection between the two, see Mac Cana, *Learned tales*, pp 146–50. On the use of Latin in medieval Irish texts and the issue of code-switching more generally, see Nicole

in *Lethech.* When the ambitious student who is being tested by Cruitíne fails to respond to the test-phrase, *Do fotha tairr tein* 'a belly from a fire is your portion', the narrator steps back to explain the significance of the phrase: the phrase is being spoken by Cruitíne's colleague to test the student who is showing worrying signs of over-confidence. The digression begins and ends with the key phrase, and then the narrative resumes in Latin: *et tribus uicibus dixit, et non respondit ei ad ullum uerbum*. It emphasizes the student's inability to respond to the extent that he can say nothing and three times he fails to respond.[27] The Latin words, however, are even more loaded. The latter phrase is used uniquely (as far as I know) in Matthew 27:14 of Christ refusing to respond to questioning by Pilate; in the Vulgate the text continues *ut miraretur praeses vehementer* 'so that the ruler marvelled greatly'. Once the text brings us to a biblical context, and in particular to the context of that part of the gospels, it is difficult to avoid being reminded of the episode in the preceding chapter of Matthew (26:69–75) when three times Peter refuses to acknowledge Christ. Peter's only reponse is *nescio quod dicis* 'I do not know what you are saying' – exactly what the student should be saying to the poet but cannot bring himself even to do that. The Latin phrase, therefore, marks an important point in the narrative, but also adds another layer of complexity and ambiguity to the story. One reading is that the student deservedly gets taken down a peg or two: this is marked verbally by the contrast between the *mórmenmae* 'over-confidence' of the student noted by Cruitíne earlier in the story and the description of the student at the end: *ba bec a menma de int éicsine* 'the confidence of the student was brought low as a result'. But the biblical resonances might suggest another reading; the context of Matthew 26–7 is one of betrayal and abandonment – Judas betrays of Christ and hangs himself; Christ is on trial, and Peter denies him three times. It is possible then that we might choose to read the student's over-confident efforts as a betrayal of trust in his teacher or alternatively that Cruitíne's efforts to deflate his student's over-confidence are a betrayal of the trust between a student and his teacher; we might think that there are other ways of letting the student down more gently. In other words, the significance of the Latin might be to set the relationship between the student and Cruitíne in a more critical light than might appear at a first reading.

A negative view of poets also underlies the *Greth* narrative involving Athairne and, in particular, the story of Senchán Torpéist in *Prull*. In the narrative as a whole, Senchán does not come out well; with his self-

Müller, 'Kodewechsel in der irischen Übersetzungsliteratur: *exempla et desiderata*' in E. Poppe and L.C.H. Tristram (eds), *Übersetzung, Adaption und Akkulteration im insularen Mittelalter* (Münster: Nodus, 1999), pp 77–86; Dagmar Bronner, 'Codeswitching in medieval Ireland: the case of the *Vita tripartita Sancti Patricii*', *Journal of Celtic linguistics*, 9 (2005), 1–12. **27** On the significance of silence

important dismissal of the possibility that anyone else could cap the verse apart from himself, he sets himself up for an inevitable fall. Not only would an audience come to this story with prejudices about Senchán firmly fixed from the kinds of stories found in the *tromdám*-style of narrative and in the importunate behaviour of high level poets such as Athairne in *Talland Étair*, but it is re-inforced by the etymology of *Torpéist* arising out of the episode where the disgustingly ugly young man succeeds in getting on as the boat was leaving Ireland for Man.[28] The poets clustering at one end of the boat, thereby almost sinking it, cry out etymologically with one voice, '*Dot·rorbai péist, a Shencháin*' '"a monster has reached you, O Senchán"', taking his name as formed from *torb-* (the prototonic stem of the verb *do·rorban*) and *péist* 'monster'). The circumstantial explanation of his name, however, also contains the negative connotations of *péist* and implications of his past behaviour as probably the most predatory of the grand poets. In addition, so appalling is the prospect of being stuck in the boat with this *gilla*, his retinue are willing to abandon Senchán, if only they could get to land; they specifically threaten him with the prospect of this *péist* being *a muinter uile* 'his whole retinue'. In legal terms, part of the definition of the status of a poet is the number in his retinue (the *SC* entry on the *ollam* (Y 998, *SC* O1) has his retinue at twenty-four), and so the consequence of Senchán being deserted by his retinue is that he would be reduced to a retinue of one, namely the ugly youth; in that respect, at least, his status would become that of a *drisiuc* as opposed to the great *fili* he is.[29] As it turns out, he retains his retinue but is subsequently reduced by his failure to cap the verses of the old woman.

The divinatory aspects of poets seem to operate as a sub-text throughout these stories. As we have seen, the poets, Lug Dall Éces and Máon mac Etna, are asked to identify the skulls of lap-dogs in *Coire Brecáin* and *Mug Éime*, respectively. In the latter, the identifying verse is produced by the process of *teinm laido*. While in the former the process is not named, it seems likely that we are to suppose that the same process was employed. Identification of remains through *teinm laido* is also used by Finn in *orc tréith* to name the owner of the headless body, the head of which was removed by Coirpre and was currently complaining at Coirpre's fireside about the lack of hospitality. Finn successfully identifies the body as that of Lomna, his fool. In the *Gaire* episode, the satire is not categorized, but in the version preserved in Dublin, Trinity College, 1363 (H.4.22), p. 8 (= *CIH* v 1587.18–1588.20) it is labelled

when speech is expected, see below, pp 31–2. **28** See now Caoimhín Ó Dónaill (ed.), *Talland Étair*. Maynooth Medieval Irish Texts, iv (Maynooth: Department of Old and Middle Irish, 2005). **29** At least according to one passage in the *Bretha Nemed*: Breatnach, *Uraicecht na ríar*, pp 20–1 (l. 54), 27 and 184.

glam díchind.[30] The *SC* entry on the third of the triad of divinatory processes, *imbas for·osnai* (Y 756, *SC* I24), is relevant at this point. While not strictly a narrative entry, it fits well with the glossary's interests in the activities of poets. John Carey has discussed this material in detail and concludes that it is only in *SC* that these practices have come together as a group and that any other source which treats them as a triad is probably to be derived from *SC*.[31] While that may be the case with regard to other later texts and is a reasonable view to take on the basis of the extant texts, such is the compilatory nature of *SC* the narratives involving divination may have ended up in *SC* by chance. On the other hand, one aim of this paper is to explore the possibility that the conjunction of a wide-range of texts on poets and poetry in *SC* may have been a deliberate process of sifting and gathering. It is certainly clear that *SC* demonstrates a keen interest in poetical matters and especially in the education and training of poets; the numerous quotations from the texts of the *Bretha Nemed*, the references to *Immacallam in dá thuarad*, and the full use of a version of a text on the grades of poets all testify to that interest.[32] A related observation can be made. First, the high density of material on poets in the shorter *SC* may well help to account for why the additional material (YAdd) has so much poetry in it; YAdd seems to consist of two discernible types of entries, short etymological entries and then entries containing quatrains exemplifying the head word. We may contrast the other early glossaries, *DDC* and *OM*, which do not show nearly the same preoccupation with poets; there is poetry but they do not contain the long narrative entries nor are they so densely packed with *Bretha Nemed*-type material.[33] In other words, it is possible that the focus on poets on *SC* is the result of a deliberate selection policy rather than being an accident of compilation.

In the early part of this paper, we have already seen individuals in these narratives who were involved in the poetico-legal sphere of satire. We began with the satire Néide mac Adnae uttered against Caíer to remove him from the kingship and we contrasted that with Coirpre Músc, who declined to use satire when his request was refused. In neither case is it immediately clear from the narratives, as they are preserved in *SC*, that satire could have been part of their armoury. In fact, in *Gaire* we only find out in the last line of the verse which concludes the story that Néide is a poet:

30 Meroney, 'Studies in early Irish satire', 215–18. **31** John Carey, 'The three things required of a poet', *Ériu* 48 (1997), 41–58; see also Joseph Nagy, 'Liminality and knowledge in the Irish tradition', *Studia Celtica* 16/17 (1981–2), 135–43 at 136–7. **32** For discussion of the input into *SC* from these sources, see Russell, 'Laws, glossaries and legal glossaries', 102–13. **33** Russell, 'Laws, glossaries and legal glossaries', 101–7.

Cloch do·rala fo chois Caíer
ro·sceind airde séolchraind súas,
do·thuit, nírbo cam in dliged,
i cend ind fhiled anúas.

A stone which was beneath the foot of Caíer
flew up a mast's height above
and fell, the principle was not wrong,
on the head of the poet from above.

However, in *Immacallam in dá thuarad* it is clear that Néide was a trained poet and so, those familiar with that text would have understood from the beginning of *Gaire* that Néide was a poet. This would explain why he could resort to satire.[34] On the other hand, at no point in *Mug Éime* are we told that Coirpre Músc is a poet, but there does seem to be some evidence that he was, assuming that he is the same individual as the Coirpre Músc mentioned in the genealogies as the fourth son of Cú Chorb of the Dál Cairpri.[35] Denied any share of his patrimony by his three brothers, he went off to Munster to seek help from his maternal grandfather, Oengus Músc.[36] The latter kept Coirpre in Munster and gave him Tír nDuais 'the land of the poet's fee' and lordship over his four uterine brothers. The reason for the former grant of land is stated explicitly: *quia poeta erat.*[37] The mid-eighth-century text, known as *Frithḟolad Muman*, on the reciprocal obligations of the people of Munster, explains that the Múscraige are to provide the *ollam* for the king of Munster because their eponymous ancestor Coirpre Músc was a poet;[38] the story preserved there is that he made a poem for Fíachu Munlethan, ancestor of all the Éoganachta, and that Clíu had been given to him as the price of the poem.[39] We may also note in passing that the female-poet in *Prull* is associated with the Múscraige. Coipre's Munster connections may also be of significance for a glossary compiled in Munster. Elsewhere in *SC*, a version of the story lying behind the genealogical story seems to be informing Y 204–5 (*SC* C1–2), where the names *Cor(b)mac* and *Coirpre* are etymologized as containing *corb .i. carpat* with the latter being analysed as *corb-aire* 'chariot-lord' or as *corb-ara* (lit.) 'chariot-charioteer'.[40] Furthermore,

34 Whitley Stokes (ed.), 'The colloquy of the two Sages', *Revue Celtique* 26 (1905), 4–64 at 14. **35** O'Brien, *Corpus*, pp 24–6 (118^b33–119^a17). **36** Matters are not helped by the tendency for the genealogists to confuse Coirpre with his grandfather. **37** O'Brien, *Corpus*, p. 26 (118b33–119a17); all the manuscripts say much the same thing in different ways; the quotation is from the Book of Leinster version; Rawlinson B 502 has *ar ba fili in Cairpri*; Lecan, *ar poeta erat uair ba filig in Cairpri sin.* **38** J.G. O'Keefe (ed.), 'Dál Caladbuig and reciprocal services between the kings of Cashel and various Munster states' in J. Fraser, P. Grosjean and J.G. O'Keefe (eds), *Irish texts*, 5 vols (London: Sheed & Ward, 1931–4), i 19–21. For discussion, see Thomas Charles-Edwards, *Early christian Ireland* (Cambridge: Cambridge University Press, 2000), pp 534–48 (esp. 542–3). **39** O'Keefe, 'Dál Caladbuig', p. 20 (§ 9). **40** On this, see Brian Ó Cuív, 'Some items from the Irish tradition', *Éigse*

the story of Coirpre Músc preserved in the genealogies is full of plays on words for chariot and charioteer. If the identification is correct and Coirpre Músc was a poet, the narrative in *Mug Éime* gains in significance in that he may have had satire in his armoury but chose not to use it when his request for the lap-dog was rejected. As we have seen, he preferred to exploit *Cáin Bretan*.

It has not been previously noticed that this law can be found elsewhere and indeed in precisely the right context, namely a law about dogs familiar to both the Irish and the British. In its Irish form in *Mug Éime* it reads: *cach bidba ina chinaid* 'every criminal [*sc.* is forfeit] for his crime'. A fuller Latin version is preserved in three distinct contexts: first, the short text, *De canibus sinodus sapientium* 'A synod of wise men: concerning dogs', contains four clauses on the legal consequences of damage by dogs or to dogs;[41] the second clause reads as follows:

> Item: canis quodlibet manducet, prima culpa nihil reddatur nisi ille solus. Si uero secundo uel tertio iterauit, reddetur quod fecerit uel commederit.
>
> Further: whatever a dog eats, let nothing be paid for his first offence except himself. If he repeats the offence a second or third time, what he does or eats it shall be paid for.

The same clause (with some minor variations) occurs in the *Collectio canonum Hibernensis* in the context of a triad *de tribus necessariis hominis* 'concerning the three necessary things of a man', which are a slave, a dog and a cow.[42] Thirdly, in the A version (but not in the P version) of the short legal text known variously as *Excerpta de libris Romanorum et Francorum* or *Canones Wallici*, the same clause occurs with almost exactly the same wording as the *Hibernensis* text.[43] While the synod text preserves the clause in a recognizable

11 (1964–6), 167–87 at 179–80; Tomás Ó Cathasaigh, *The heroic biography of Cormac mac Airt* (Dublin: DIAS, 1977), pp 43–8 (esp. 44). **41** Ludwig Bieler (ed.), *The Irish penitentials*, Scriptores Latini Hibernici, v (Dublin: Dublin Institute for Advanced Studies, 1975), pp 174–5 (Irish Canons, vi) (and pp 8–9 for a brief discussion); see also James F. Kenney, *The sources for the early history of the Irish church: ecclesiastical. An introduction and guide* (New York: Columbia University Press, 1929), p. 244. The third and fourth clauses have been discussed by Liam Breatnach, 'On the glossing of early Irish law-texts, fragmentary texts, and some aspects of the law relating to dogs' in A. Ahlqvist, G.W. Banks et al. (eds), *Celtica Helsingensia. Proceedings from a symposium on Celtic studies*, Commentationes Humanarum Litterarum, 107 (Helsinki: Societas Scientiarum Fennica, 1996), pp 11–20 at 15–20. On the surviving fragments of the Irish law on dogs, see Breatnach, *Companion*, 301–2. **42** Hermann Wasserschleben (ed.), *Die irische Kanonensammlung* (2nd ed., Leipzig: Tauchnitz, 1885; repr. 1966), p. 214 (LIII.6). **43** Bieler, *Irish penitentials*, pp 148–9 (§62); for the manuscript sigla, see ibid., pp 12–16. For a recent discussion of the *Excerpta* which usefully discusses the previous scholarship on this text, see Morfydd E. Owen, 'The *Excerpta de Libris Romanorum et Francorum* and Welsh law' in T.M. Charles-Edwards and P. Russell (eds), *Tair colofn cyfraith. The three columns of law in medieval Wales: homicide, theft and fire* (Bangor: Welsh Legal History Society, 2007), pp 171–95.

context of dog-law, in the *Hibernensis* only the first two clauses are found, and in the *Excerpta* the clause stands alone at the end of the *A* version.[44] In both of these texts, then, the regulation on dogs appears to be a secondary addition. The fullest version preserved in the synod text seems to be in an Irish context; and in the light of Breatnach's demonstration that the third and fourth clauses can be related to the story of how Cú Chulainn got his name, it would seem deeply embedded in that context.[45] However, given that the wording of these different versions is not identical, it is possible that the versions in the *Hibernensis* and *Excerpta* are derived from a slightly different version than that preserved in the synod.[46] It is also worth drawing attention both to the Breton provenance of manuscript B (Paris, BN, Latin MS 3182) which contains this synod text and to the arguable Breton affinities of many of the manuscripts of the *Collectio canonum Hibernensis*.[47] In particular, the version of the synod text in manuscript B contains an Old Breton gloss, *buorth*, glossing *bouello* 'cow-shed' and that the same gloss, in the form *buuoort* glossing *bobello*, is found in the equivalent passage of the *Hibernensis* in several manuscripts.[48] The connection is circumstantial but may be significant. More generally, our text seems to have travelled in the kind of company which would allow it to be known on both sides of the Irish Sea and also in Brittany. Whatever its origin, it seems that in Irish circles by the ninth or tenth century this law was thought of as peculiar to the British (which should perhaps be taken to include the Bretons). According to this regulation, while the animal itself is forfeit for a first offence, second and third offences by the same animal involve the payment of extra compensation. Coirpre was of course not interested in whether the dog would re-offend; the first offence gave him what he wanted, the dog itself.

The other interesting aspect is why it is is called a *cáin*, a term used both for ecclesiastical and secular regulations and laws.[49] The canonical context of

44 Subsequently, it appears that another clause (§63) on being kicked by a beast was added. **45** Breatnach 'On the glossing of early Irish law-texts', pp 15–20. **46** The versions in the *Hibernensis* and the *Excerpta* with minor variations agree against the version in the synod *de canibus*: the main difference is that the former make the second sentence active with *dominus* as the subject as against the impersonal of the synod text. **47** For discussion, see Owen, '*Excerpta*'. **48** For the two occurrences of this gloss, see respectively Bieler, *Irish penitentials*, p. 174, n. to line 20 (his reading is *buorch*), and Wasserschleben, *Die irische Kanonensammlung*, p. 214, n. d; for discussion of the gloss, see Whitley Stokes, 'Old Breton glosses', *Revue celtique* 4 (1879–80), 324–48 at 328 and 346; Léon Fleuriot and Claude Evans, *A dictionary of Old Breton*, 2 vols (Toronto: Prepcorp, 1985), vol. 1, pp 92 and 331. Wasserschleben notes the gloss in two manuscripts of the *Hibernensis*, Paris, BN, Latin MSS 12021 and 3182 (this also containing the synod text), but, according to Fleuriot, it is also to be found in London, BL, Cotton MS, Otho E.xiii. I am grateful to Roy Flechner for help on this point. **49** On *cána*, see Thomas Charles-Edwards, *The early medieval Gaelic lawyer*. Quiggin pamphlet on the sources of mediaeval Gaelic history, 4 (Cambridge: Department of Anglo-Saxon, Norse, and Celtic, 1999), pp 43–61; Charles-Edwards, *Early Christian Ireland*, pp 559–69; Breatnach,

the synod text and the general ecclesiastical context of its quotation in the *Hibernensis* might help, even though, as Bieler notes, there is nothing particularly ecclesiastical about the synod *de canibus*.[50] Most *cána* are attributed to a named individual, e.g. *Cáin Adomnáin* etc., but *Cáin Bretan* seems to be attributed to a people. It cannot mean the 'law over the Britons' as that was usually expressed with the preposition *for*, but seems to mean a law promulgated by the British.[51] It is also not clear precisely who the *Bretain* are in this context. Coirpre has gone to visit his kinsmen and friends in Britain and while among them he invokes *Cáin Bretan*. In other words, the context is not the British themselves, but the Irish living in Britain. Either we have to assume it was possible by the ninth or tenth century to use *Bretain* to refer to the Irish living in Britain, as well as to the British themselves, or it was possible for the Irish to assume that the Irish living in Britain in this earlier period had lived under British law, a law which they felt comfortable calling a *cáin*.

There are some loose ends here, but even so it seems that in *Mug Éime* we have a narrative, aspects of which criss-cross the Irish Sea in a number of ways. We have Coirpre Músc, an individual with Munster associations, set in the context of Irish contacts with Britain, and especially with the Britons of Cornwall who inhabited *Dún mac Líathain*, the British version of which is given to us as *Din map Letain*, thus reminding us that not only did these contacts involve legal matters, but linguistic ones as well.[52] When Coirpre crossed over to Britain to visit friends and family (and the tenses indicate that this was a regular journey), on one trip he returned with the first lap-dog to have reached Ireland and gained the dog by recourse to a law which itself seems to have travelled between Ireland and Britain.

I have discussed aspects of the interest in legal matters in *SC* elsewhere. Again in part it seems to be the case that the compilers had access to a considerable number of glossaries (or indeed sections of glossaries) based on legal texts. Such glossaries have survived independently, such as the single folio of a glossary to *Bretha nemed déidenach* preserved in TCD MS 1337 (H.3.18), pp 61–2 (= *CIH* ii 603.16–604.38) or pre-eminently O'Davoren's Glossary. The Munster focus of many of the sources of *SC* may be sufficient to account for proportionally high number of entries deriving from texts associated with the *Bretha Nemed*. Even so, as we have seen, *SC* is pre-occupied with satire and poets. Another legal aspect is worth considering here as it seems to lie behind some of the narratives is an interest in precious objects. One of the legal texts which *SC* seems to have exploited (probably via a text glossary) is a text on pledges from *Bretha nemed toísech* (*CIH* vi

Companion, pp 191–202. **50** Bieler, *Irish penitentials*, p. 9. **51** See the examples from the annals, noted by Charles-Edwards, *The early medieval Gaelic lawyer*, p. 47 (III.4). **52** See Russell, 'Brittonic words'.

2223.18–33) which has provided material for a number of entries. The point of the original text seems to be that a person should make a pledge with an item which is of particular value or significance to him, often related to his profession; thus *nasc deobuire dodaile fimm i crethir cim uim oll nos nuim puicirne puinc puincne* (*CIH* 2223.31–2) 'the pledge (*nasc*) of a cup-bearer who pours wine into a drinking-cup: (?) silver around an *ól*-measure of milk or around a notched balance'.[53] The text from *cim* onwards is quoted Y 304, *SC* C101 *cim* (also *DDC* C14). This interest in valuable objects may again be related to the chance occurrence of particular types of text on the compiler's desk, but throughout *SC* entries on vessels and valuable objects occur, and they are also the focus of attention in some of the narrative entries: a valuable knife is the object of the request in *Gaire* which gives rise to the satire, and similarly a knife is the means to an end in *Mug Éime*. It is worth pointing out that, since the headwords in the early glossaries are with one exception much more nominal than verbal (in *O'Dav* a good proportion of the head-words are verb-forms), one might expect there to be references to objects. Even with that proviso, the concern with objects is striking. It is perhaps no surprise then that two of the longer entries in *SC* have to do with merchants, *cendaigi*, trading between Britain, Ireland, Scotland and Man: Manannán mac Lir, who took his name from the Isle of Man, and Brecán mac Maine of the Uí Néill, who was sucked into Coire Brecáin. Such merchants may well have been trading to and fro with precisely these kinds of objects in their holds. Manannán and Brecán also seem to illustrate two aspects of the same activity. While Manannán is the best helmsman in the western world and therefore a highly successful merchant who is thought to possess divine knowledge of the unreliable weather conditions of the Irish Sea, Brecán is by implication less successful since he contrived to get himself swallowed by the eponymous whirlpool, the terrors of which are described for us in impressive detail.[54] An important aspect of the perception of successful merchants as quasi-divine is that they can control the weather and tides and so succeed in those liminal areas of the world where strange things can happen.

That much of the action in the longer narratives in *SC* takes place in such liminal areas or involves crossing boundaries of one sort or another is in one sense simply to observe that these narratives deal with the same kinds of themes as occur elsewhere in early Irish narrative. Even so, within these

53 The translation tentatively suggested above for the second part is based on reading the text as *cim im ól n-aiss no im puincirne puincne* 'silver around an *ól*-measure of milk or around a notched balance', where *ól n-aiss* refers to a vessel of that particular size. The same text is quoted in *O'Dav* 1609 *uim*.
54 For discussion of the description of the whirlpool and the parallels to the description of Scylla and Charybdis, see Jacqueline Borsje, *From chaos to enemy: encounters with monsters in early Irish texts. An investigation related to the process of christianization and the concept of evil*. Instrumenta patristica, xxix (Turnhout: Brepols, 1996), p. 54.

stories it remains an important theme. We have already mentioned merchants, but it also the case that a number of significant episodes occur on sea-shores; the skull of Brecán's lap-dog is found at Inber Bec and only by this is his death known; in *Prull* not only is the female poet first encountered on the shore of Man and the whole process of discovery takes place there, but the encounters with the Spirit of Poetry (in both ugly and beautiful guises) which frame the narrative take place on the shore of Ireland before and after thr trip to Man. Moving inland, in both *Greth* and *Lethech*, the key players Athairne and Cruitíne lurk on the edges of the narrative: Cruitíne is said to have concealed himself *i maig*, and we are to assume that Athairne is not far off – both seem to be in the marginal and liminal territory just out beyond the domesticated environs of the house. When in *Gaire* Néide finally repents of his actions in driving Caíer away and goes to seek him out, the final scenes of Caíer's death and the disfigurement of Néide take place *fond licc íar cúl in dúine fo scailp* 'beneath a rock in a cleft behind the fortress' where Caíer has hidden, exactly where Néide's verse had predicted: *fo ró, fu mara, fu chara* 'under earth, under ramparts, under stones'; it is just outside the fortress but neither above nor below ground. Joseph Nagy has explored the implications of this liminality in greater detail than I can here;[55] he has noted the liminality of the activities described in *imbas for·osnai*, the liminal nature of the lap-dog, and chronological liminality of the *gilla* as neither boy nor man. In particular he has focused on the liminality of Finn and his men, and it is striking that almost all the crucial moments of *Orc tréith* occur in these liminal places: Coirpre lies with Finn's woman and is spotted by Lomna, Finn's fool, when he is wandering *ammuigh* 'outside'. Similarly, the episode where Lomna's head utters a string of dire threats is located at one of the Fenian cooking-sites where they are cooking fish over the fire, already a liminal place, but then, when his threats become too objectionable, Coirpre orders the head to be put *amach* 'away, out', that is, even further away. Throughout these stories the use of *amaig*, *i maig* etc. is striking; such words imply a distance away from the normal sphere of human activity, whether it is in the undergrowth outside a house or the fortress or away from the warmth and hospitality of the cooking-fire.

The final theme to emerge from this study has to do with language. In almost all these stories, the turning-point of the narrative is expressed in complex and obscure language, sometimes in verse, but often in alliterative runs of prose. Both lap-dog skulls are identified in verse as is Lomna's headless body by Finn. Likewise, in *Gaire* in addition to the satire being in verse, the denouement of the narrative is also in verse, *ut dixit poeta*, which follows Néide's uttering such an impenetrable phrase, *'ní cúala cuic núin'* 'You

55 Nagy, 'Liminality'.

did not hear an evil secret' (?), that elements of it figure as headwords in their own right elsewhere in *SC* and elsewhere.[56] In *Prull* the quatrains of verse and the inability on the part of Senchán to complete them are precisely the point of the whole narrative. As we have seen, in both *Greth* and *Lethech* the inability to understand what is said sits at the core of the narrative: Greth is unable to understand what is said to him by Amairgen and it is by that incomprehensible utterance that Amairgen is recognized by Athairne. In *Lethech* the ambitious apprentice poet is put in his place by failing to understand the deliberately obscure words of Cruitíne's colleague which turn out in the end to be no more complex than a set of instructions straight out of a recipe for boiled belly-pork; it is reasonable to assume that the disparity between the high-flown language and the mundane content is part of the point being made to the apprentice. In *Orc tréith* Lomna's severed head is also concerned with cooking;[57] his complex utterances are triggered by Coirpre and his men failing to give him his proper portion of grilled fish. Even when the head is taken elsewhere, the voice can still be heard uttering threats and promises of doom and catastrophe. In this case, the issue of language is less that Coirpre and his men do not understand what he is saying so much as they refuse to listen. Their doom is spelt out before them, but they choose not to hear. More importantly, they have broken the rules of hospitality by not feeding his head; it is stated very clearly that this was a *géis* for Finn. Lomna can thus say *ro rannais rand nad cert* 'you have made a division which is not fair' and this is one of the themes of the whole story. There is of course an ambiguity as to which *rann* is not fair – Lomna's head seems to be referring to the division of the fish and the consequent abuse of hospitality, but more importantly he is also referring to the division of Lomna into his constituent parts of head and body. In other narratives in *SC*, the interest in language seems less pressing, but even in *Mug Éime* there is a digression on the Irish and British words for 'son' (*mac* and *map* respectively), and in *Imbas for·osnai* there is a reference to chanting at various stages of the ritual, even though we are given no indication of what is said. In many cases, these utterances are very difficult to interpret and it may well be that we are missing many of the nuances; for example, in *Gaire* when Néide, surrounded

56 Cf. *SC* C100 *Cuic .i. rún, ut Néde mac Adna dixit, 'ní chúala cuic núin,' ol mé, 'Caíar gáir'* '*Coic* "secret, advice", i.e. secret, *as* Néide mac Adnae *said*, "You did not hear an evil secret", I said, "short-lived Caíer"'; *núin*: glosses on *Bretha Nemed Déidenach, nuin .i. olc, ut est ni cuala coic .n. .i. ni cuala arma run olc damh* (*CIH* ii, 603.31) '*núin*, i.e. evil, thus it is "you have not heard an evil secret", i.e. "you have not heard", said I, "an evil secret from me"'; also *Immacallam in dá thúarad*, X.6 (Stokes, 'The colloquy of the two Sages', 14) where it is spoken by Ferchetne to Néide mac Adnae: *ni chuala cuic n-inne maicc Adnai*; Stokes translated 'I never heard the secret of the sense of Adnae's son' (note the potential minim confusion between *núin* and *n-inne*) **57** On the importance of cooking and the cooking-pit, see Nagy, *Wisdom of the outlaw*, pp 132–5.

by all the trappings of Caíer's power, his wife, chariot and hunting-dog, is spotted approaching Dún Cermnai, where Caíer had taken refuge, Caíer remarks *'Batar sin do·ríadatar a fochlai fria faitsi'* 'They are those who rode from the north towards the south', to which Cacher mac Etarscél says, 'That is the word of a king'.[58] Why those words are particularly diagnostic of royalty remain unclear. In some case, however, it is the very fact that they are in a different register which is sufficient to mark them out. More generally in *SC*, in addition to the broad interest about where words come from, there is a striking sensitivity to different types of language. For example, in the entry on *nairne*, a sense of regional and chronological variation is displayed:[59]

> *SC* Y 792: Nairne .i. glaine. Nó nairne amail bid naire no beth and .i. senbérla didiu in naire n-í sin. Is inand 7 as·bertha écin. Is gnáthbérla ísem tra cid indiu la h-Írmumain maxime, unde dicitur: 'in fil ní bas toich duit?' 'Fil naire', ol intí dia n-imchomarcar .i. fil écin.
>
> *Nairne*, i.e. 'purity'. Or *nairne* as if it were *naire*, i.e. that *naire* is old-fashioned language then. It is the same as would be said *écin* (indeed). It is the usual language even today in West Munster especially; whence is said: 'Is there anything which is pleasing to you?'. 'There is, indeed (*naire*)', says the one of whom the question is asked, i.e. there is, indeed (*écin*).

What is current in West Munster (*gnáthbérla*) is old-fashioned and out of date (*senbérla*) among the sophisticates of East Munster. In *cloch*, on the other hand, where three different words for 'stone' are presented, we seem to have moved into the differentiation by register: *SC* Y 213 *Cloch, trí anmann lé .i. onn a íarmbérla, cloch a gnáthbérla, cloech a bérla n-airberta ar inní chlóes cach raod* '*cloch* (stone), three names for it: *onn* the cryptic term for it, *cloch* the normal term for it, *cloech* the term of use for it because it blunts everything'. Particularly noteworthy is *onn* which is described as *íarmbérla*, a term which has its own entry elsewhere: *SC* Y 755 *Iarnnbérlae .i. is aire is·berar, ar a duibe in bélrae ar a dorchatae ar a dlúithe, co nach erasa taisscelad ind* '*Iarnnbérlae*: it is on account of this it is so called, on account of the darkness of the language and on account of its obscurity and its denseness, so that it is not easy to examine it'. These smaller entries give us a context within the glossary for thinking about the obscure and difficult passages within the longer narratives. It becomes possible then to think of such passages almost as exercises in *íarmbérla*, and again the possibility emerges that these entries did not arrive in *SC* by accident, but as part of a more general selection of material.[60]

58 The interpretation of Caíer's utterance follows suggestions made by David Greene, 'Varia II: 5. *faitse, fochlae*', *Ériu* 21 (1969), 94–8. **59** For discussion of this entry, see Paul Russell, '"What was best of every language": the early history of the Irish language' in D. Ó Cróinín (ed.), *A new history of Ireland*, vol. 1 (Oxford: Oxford University Press, 2005), pp 405–50 at 439–40. **60** The issue of

The converse of speech is silence, and there are some notable moments in these stories where unexpected silences occur. In *Prull* Senchán is explicitly reduced to silence by his inability to cap the verses of the old woman:

> Sochtaid íarum Senchán 7 ind écis uile dano. Do·ling íarum in gillae remeperta ar béulu Sencháin 7 as·bert: 'Tá, a chaillech! Na·accaille Senchán! Ní comadus dit. Atom·gláide-sa amne, ol nít·acelldadar nach aile don muinter-se.'
>
> Senchán grows silent then, as do all the poets. Then the aforementioned lad leaps out in front of Senchán and said, 'Silent, woman! Do not address Senchán! It is not fitting for you. Address me in this way, since no other from this retinue will address you'.

The scabrous young man interrupts by leaping in front of Senchán; significantly the phrase is *ar béulu Sencháin*, which in spatial terms naturally means 'in front of Senchán', though given the eventual identity of the young man, it may contain the implication of taking precedence by right; more literally, however, and more importantly in this context, it can be take to mean 'on the lips of'. The young man's words are loaded with speaking words: his first word to the woman is *tá* 'be silent', followed by three different forms of *ad·gládathar, na·accaille … atom·gláide-sa … nít·acelldadar*. From then on, until he realizes who the woman is, Senchán remains silent. His sudden interjection of recognition (when we had almost forgotten he was still there) has the air of a desperate attempt to regain the initiative. We have also seen how in a similar way Greth and Cruitíne's ambitious student were reduced to silence by the complexity and sophistication of language. In contrast, not even decapitation can silence Lomna, while Coirpre and his men by implication remain silent or are indeed silenced by the stream of words from Lomna's head. Robin Chapman Stacey has recently drawn attention to the nuances of speech and silence in the context of performance of the law in early Ireland; she draws attention to the correlation between silence and subordination on the one hand and between speech and power on the other.[61] Despite his power, Senchán is reduced to silence and to a subordinate position by his inability to cap the verses, while the position of the young man is

register in early Irish needs much more discussion than can be devoted to it here; we may compare, for example, *Auraicept na nÉces*: *it é cóic gné bérla tóbaidi .i. bérla Féne 7 fasaige na filed 7 bérla etarscarta 7 bérla fortchide na filed tríasa n-agallit cach dib a chéle 7 íarmbérla* 'there are five types of chosen language: the language of the Irish, the sayings of the poets, the separated language, the concealed language of the poets by which they speak to each other, and obscure (*or* unaccented) language' (George Calder (ed.), *Auraicept na n-éces* (Edinburgh: John Grant, 1917), p. 100 (ll. 1302–4) (cf. also p. 244 (ll. 4619–21). Cf. also some of the comments in Russell, '"What was best of every language"', pp 439–50. **61** Stacey, *Dark Speech*, pp 138–9.

raised by his ability to speak. Furthermore, his forceful silencing of the old woman reinforces his position of power: 'If silence equals subordination, and speech … was for many a manner in which to claim superior standing in a relationship, then an important aspect of enjoining silence on one party by another was the assertion of authority over that person'.[62] The interesting point about the *Prull* narrative is that, despite our suspicions, we only discover the basis of the young man's power in the last line of the story, and that, as we have noted, is in Latin. The episode of the over-confident student also gains in impact from being considered in this light. He is reduced to silence because he cannot understand or indeed produce language of the appropriate register. In that respect he is not dissimilar to low-ranking poets discussed by Stacey who repeat *roscada* by rote but cannot compose them for themselves.[63] On the other hand, it is not clear whether we are supposed to think that Greth, as Athairne's *gilla*, ought to understand what is being said to him by Amairgen. This depends partly on what we think *gilla* means; as Nagy has shown, it can mean 'servant', but also 'student' or 'pupil', and strikingly entries interpreting it in both ways are found in *SC* (Y 676, *SC* G7 and YAdd 702, *SC* G33, respectively).[64] If the latter sense is intended in *Greth*, this comes closer to the *Lethech* episode, where the over-confident student is deliberately exposed and deflated. If Athairne's *gilla* is a student, then perhaps we may contrast his behaviour with that of Cruitíne's student: while the latter thinks too highly of his own abilities, the former is willing to acknowledge that he does not know what the young Amairgen is saying.

This paper has been a heuristic exercise in seeing what would happen if we assumed that the longer narratives in *SC* were in some way linked. It has not provided complete readings of each story and it has meandered from one to another in a rather aimless way. Neither has any systematic attempt been made to compare the versions of the narrative in *SC* with variant versions preserved elsewhere outside the glossaries. The aim has been to consider them as a group and to see what dynamic arises out of them. Much work remains to be done on the individual narratives, but by treating them as a group, it does appear that sufficiently interesting themes and links have emerged to justify the approach. In many cases, such an approach highlights aspects of these narratives which have not been identified by other scholars; that is not to say that one approach is right and another wrong, but rather to observe that these tales permit a multiplicity of complementary analyses and interpretations. What it may tell us about the interests of the compilers of *SC* at various stages in its compilation is a different matter. When set against the background of the shorter entries it is at least arguable that one of the main

62 Ibid., p. 139. **63** Ibid., pp 210–11; cf. also Breatnach, *Uraicecht na ríar*, p. 113 (§18), on the *taman*. **64** Nagy, *Wisdom of the outlaw*, pp 125–6.

preoccupations of the compilers of the shorter SC was the activity of poets in the broadest sense – their status, their education and, in particular, the types of language which they had to master in order to be a poet.

APPENDIX
The longer narratives from *Sanas Cormaic*

The following translations are provided to support the reading of the above paper. It should be noted that they are provisional and liberally sprinkled with question marks. It is hoped that by the time the full edition of *SC* appears, some of the difficulties will have been resolved.

Note: italicized text is in Latin in the original; text in [ ] provides the etymological analysis implied in the text.

Coire Brecáin (Y 323 = *SC* C122)
Coire Brecáin, i.e., a great whirlpool which is between Ireland and Scotland to the north, i.e. a meeting place of many seas: the sea which comes round Ireland from the north-west, and the sea which comes round Scotland from the north-east, and the sea from the south between Ireland and Scotland. Then it takes them each in turn like whirling spirals and puts each of them in the place of the other like the paddles of a mill-wheel as it goes past, and sucks them down into the depths so that it is like an open-mouthed cauldron which would suck down even the whole of Ireland, and would put it in all together. Again it vomits up that mouthful and its thunderous belching and its crashing and its roaring can be heard among the clouds just like a cauldron boiling on the fire.

Brecán then was a famous merchant of the Uí Néill who had fifty currachs trading between Ireland and Scotland. They happened upon that whirlpool and it swallowed them all up together, and no-one survived from it to bring news of their destruction.[65]

Brecán, the son of Maine, son of Níall of the nine hostages, so another book says, used to come there, and he had fifty currachs trading between Ireland and Scotland, and they fell into that cauldron on one occasion, and no-one survived to bring news of their destruction,[66] and their death was not known until Lugaid Dall-éces came to Bangor. His company came to the strand of Inber Bec, and they found there a small bare skull. They took it with them to Lugaid. *They questioned him about whose it was and he said to them*, i.e. his company asked who it was and he said to them, 'Put the end of

65 This paragraph is only in the M and Y-group versions; La is missing at this point. **66** This paragraph up to this point is only in the B and Y-group versions; La is missing at this point.

the poet's staff upon it'. That was done, *and* Lugaid *said*, 'A wretched death from the deep sea has Brecán died by water or by whirlpool. That is the head of Brecán's lap-dog, and this is a small thing from something great', he said, 'for Brecán with all his company has been drowned in yonder whirlpool'.

Gaileng (Y 685 = *SC* G16)
Gaeleng (name), [< *gae* 'spear' + *lang* 'treacherous'] i.e. treacherous spear, i.e. excrement on honour, i.e. it was applied to Cormac mac Taidg mac Céin. He made a feast for Tadg, i.e. for his father with a hundred of every kind of animal at it except badgers alone. Then Cormac went to a badgers' set. He thought it slow to wait for it to be destroyed, so he called them out under the protection of the honour of his father, Tadg. The badgers came. Cormac killed them then, a hundred of them, and he displayed them at the feast, and the heart of Tadg shuddered at it and he refused it. Afterwards he found out what had been done there, and he named his son *from this name*, i.e. Cormac Gaileng, from whom the Gaileng take their name. Gaileng, i.e. [< *gáu* 'falsehood' + *lang* 'treacherous'] treacherous falsehood, i.e. without a transaction. Gaileng, then, i.e. [< *gal* 'ardour' or ? *gáel* 3 'wound' + *seng* 'thin'] thin ardour (or wound), on account of the fact that each one of them grew thin.

Gaire (Y 698 = *SC* G29)[67]
Gaire 'short life', i.e. short life, [< *gair* 'short' + *ré* 'period of time'], i.e. short time, as in the satire which Néide mac Adnae meic Gutháir made against the king of Connacht, i.e. against the brother of his own father, i.e. for Caíer mac Gutháir, i.e. Caíer adopted Néide as his son, since he did not have a son besides. Caíer's wife fell in love with Néide, and gave Néide a silver apple as a sign of her love. Néide did not accept it until she promised the kingship to him after him (*sc.* Caíer) if he went to her. 'How will we achieve this?', asked Néide. 'Not difficult', said the woman, 'Make a satire against him so that there will be a defect on him. A man with a defect will not hold the kingship'. 'I will not get a refusal from him. The man will not give me a refusal. There is nothing in his possession in the world which he will not give to me'. 'I know', she said, 'something that he will not give to you, i.e. the knife he was given in the lands of Alba, he will not give that to you. It is a prohibition for him that it be taken from him'.

Néide asked Caíer for the knife. 'Alas! It is a prohibition for me that it be taken from me!' Néide performed a *glám dícend* against him, and three blisters appeared on his cheeks. This is the satire:

67 This full version is only preserved in the Y-group versions; versions B and M contain only the satire and the glosses on it, and La is missing at this point.

> Evil, death, short life for Caíer,
> The spears of battle will wound him, Caíer.
> May Caíer die! may Caíer perish! Caíer
> under earth, under ramparts, under stones.

Maile then, i.e. evil, from *malum*; *baire*, i.e. death; *gaire*, i.e. short life; *Caíeur*, i.e. for Caíer; *cealtra catha*, i.e. spears, whence is it said *díchealtair*, i.e. a spear-shft without a metal tip on it. *Fu ró*, i.e. *fo úr* 'under clay', i.e. transposition of letters; *fo mara*, i.e. under lofty, green ramparts; *fo chara*, i.e. under stones.

Caíer arose early in the morning and went to the well. He put his hand across his face. He found three blisters on his face; the satire had made them, i.e. blemish, defect, and deficiency, i.e. red and blue and white.[68] Caíer fled so that no one would look upon him in disgrace, until he was in Dún Cermnae with Cacher mac Etarscél.

Néide took the kingship of Connacht after him. And he ruled until the end of the year. He regretted the torment of Caíer. Néide went after him to Dún Cermnae in the chariot of Caíer and the wife of Caíer with him and his hunting hound. 'It is a fine charioteer who approaches the fortress. His appearance reveals how his splendour was. Who is that?', said everyone. Caíer said, 'They are those who rode from the north towards the south', i.e. *fochla* is the *name* of warrior's seat in the chariot. *Faitsi* is the name of the seat of the charioteer. *Fochla* then is every noble seat. *Faitsi* every front seat. 'That is the word of a king', said Cacher mac Etarscél. He did not realise until then. 'Alas for my soul!', said Caíer. With that Caier turned away from them until he was under a stone in a cleft behind the fortress. Néide came in his chariot to the fortress. The hounds picked up Caíer's trail and found him under the stone behind the fortress. Caíer died from shame at seeing Néide. The rock boiled and blazed at the death of Caíer and a splinter flew from the rock into the eye of Néide and shattered in his head. As a result, Néide said, 'You did not hear an evil secret', etc. *As said a poet*:

> A stone which was beneath the foot of Caíer
> flew up a mast's height above
> and fell, the principle was not wrong,
> on the head of the poet from above.

Greth (Y 690 = *SC* G21)[69]

Greth (personal name), the name of the servant (or student) of Athairne, *to whom* Amargein, son of Ecet Salach, the smith from Búais, *spoke*. The servant

68 On the multicolour blemishes, see Meroney, 'Studies in early Irish satire', 223–6. **69** This full version is only preserved in the Y-group versions; versions B and M contain only the quotation of Amairgen's words, and La is missing at this point.

of Amargein went to the house of Ecet Salach, the smith, to seek a loan and he saw the infant by the fire, and he was no greater than a fist, but he was, however, a full seven years old. He was at that time gnawing wild garlic and curds etc. Then he said to Greth, 'Does Greth eat curds (i.e. cooked), blackberries (?), sloes (?), sprigs of wild garlic, pine-nuts (i.e. nuts), sour (?) apples, curds? Does Greth eat curds?'

Then the servant related that to Athairne. Athairne came with an axe in his hand to kill him (*sc.* the infant). The father of the boy came in the nick of time and asked the daughter, 'Who has come to the house?' The girl said, 'The servant of Athairne came', and related what had happened. 'Well, indeed', said his father, 'Athirne will come and kill the boy. Conceal the boy,' he said, 'and place his clothes where he is'. It was done thus. Athairne came and gave a blow to the block of wood in the clothing. The daughter raised the alarm then and he fled.

This is the redress which was given then for it: the boy to be taught for Ecet Salach, the smith, until he was no worse in skill than Athairne. Then Amargein was brought to him.

Imbas for·osnai (Y 756 = *SC* I24)

Imbas for·osnai, i.e. it reveals whatever thing the poet likes and what he desires to be revealed. It is carried out as follows: the poet chews on a piece of raw meat of a pig or dog or cat, and he puts it on a flagstone behind the door, and he chants a spell over it, and offers it to the pagan gods, and he calls them to him, and he does not leave it on the next day. Then he chants over his two palms, and he summons pagan gods to him so that his sleep be not disturbed, and he puts his two palms around his two cheeks, and falls asleep. There are usually people watching over him so that he should not turn over and that no-one should disturb him. And that which is in store for him is revealed to him for a period of nine days or twice that or three times that, for however long he should estimate at the offering. And thus it is called *imbas*, [< *imm* 'around' + *bas* 1 'palm of the hand'], i.e. a palm on this side and a palm on that around his head.

Patrick had banished that and *teinm laído*, and he declared that anyone who will do it should not be of heaven or earth; for it is a denial of baptism. However, as for *díchetal dí chennaib*, that has been left as a proper part of the art; for science causes that, and there is no need for them to make offering to the demons, but a declaration from the ends of bones at once.

Lethech (Y 825 = *SC* L33)

Lethech, i.e. it has two meanings: first, [< *leithe* 1 'breadth'] a name for a kind of fish which is called *lethech* on account of its breadth and its thinness, for it is as broad as anything which is in the ocean. Secondly, [< *lethaid* 'spread, flatten'] a name for a trough because bread dough is spread out on it, as Cruitíne, the poet, said. One day he came to the house of another poet and a lad with him, i.e. an apprentice who had the ambition to be a teacher. Cruitíne concealed himself outside and sent the lad to the house of the poet to seek hospitality. A belly of a boar was given to him in a cauldron and meanwhile the poet talked to the apprentice keeping an eye on his application. The poet recognised the arrogance of the apprentice and the smallness of his application. When the belly-meat was cooked, the poet said in front of the apprentice, 'A belly from a fire is your portion', i.e. it is time to take it from the fire. It was so that he might find out what answer the apprentice would give to him; for he had heard the apprentice boasting falsely about his various, wondrous inventions as if it was he himself who had invented them, and he did not believe the apprentice. It was for this reason that the poet said to test the apprentice, 'A belly from a fire is your portion', *and three times he spoke, and he* (sc. *the apprentice*) *did not reply to a single word of it.*

With that, the apprentice got up and went out to where Cruitíne was, and related the story to him, and he told him what the poet had said to him, i.e. 'a belly from a fire is your portion'. 'Well', said Cruitíne, 'when he says it again, you answer him with this, "Turn a trough flat against it; light a candle", i.e. put a trough flat against it, i.e. under the belly and let a candle serve to see whether the belly is cooked'.

When the apprentice went back into the house, the poet *said* the same thing and the apprentice *said* the same, 'put a trough flat under it, etc.' 'Well then', said the poet, 'the stomach of an apprentice did not speak thus. Cruitíne is nearby; call him in!' He was summoned then. He was welcomed and other food was put into the cauldron for him, and as a result the confidence of the apprentice was very low because the poet had ridiculed him until Cruitíne spoke to him.

Manannán mac Lir (Y 896 = *SC* M46)

Manannán mac Lir, he was a wonderful merchant in the Isle of Man. He was the best helmsman in the western world. He would know through his knowledge of the weather, i.e. by examining the aspect of the sky, i.e. of the atmosphere, how long the good weather and the bad weather would last and when each one of the periods would change. *As a result the Irish and the Britons called him a god of the sea, and so said that he was the son of the sea,* i.e. mac Lir. From the name of the Isle of Man he was called Mannanán.

Mug Éime (Y 883 = *SC* M33)

Mug Éime [< *mug* 'slave, servant' + *em* 'hilt'], the name of the first lap-dog which was first in Ireland, i.e. Coirpre Músc brought it to Ireland from

Britain. For when the power of the Irish over the Britons was great, they divided Britain between then into territories, and each knew the dwelling of his friend, and the Irish dwelt by the sea in the east no less than in Ireland. Their dwellings and royal forts were built there.

Thus is called Din Tradui, i.e. fort of the triple ramparts, i.e. the triple ramparts of Crimthann Mór mac Fidaig, king of Ireland and Britain as far as the English Channel. And thus is Glastonbury of the Irish, i.e. a church on the edge of the English Channel. That was the dwelling where Glass mac Caiss was, swineherd of the king of Irúait, with his pigs feeding on mast. It is he whom Patrick resurrected after a time, i.e. one hundred and twenty years after he was killed by the *fiana* of Mac Con, etc. And from that division the Din Map Letain is still in the lands of the Britons of Cornwall, i.e. the Fort of the sons of Líathan; for in British *map* means 'son'. Thus each tribe made a division so that there was an equal amount in the east, and those lands were under that power for some considerable time after the coming of Patrick.

As a result of that, Coirpre Músc was visiting his family and friends in the east. At that time a lap-dog has not come to Ireland, and it was proclaimed by the Britons that no lap-dog should be taken to Ireland as a request or as a gift, nor in friendship nor by barter with the Irish. There was a law among the Britons at that time: 'the criminal for his crime to the one whose law he shall have impugned'. There was a beautiful lap-dog in the possession of a friend of Coirpre Músc in Britain and Coirpre could not get it from him. Then Coirpre came one day to that man's house and was made welcome to everything but the lap-dog. Coirpre Músc had a fine knife, with working of gold and silver around its hilt; it was a wonderful possession. Coirpre put lots of grease around its hilt and rubbed bacon fat and beef fat on it. He left the knife in front of the lap-dog. The lap-dog then chewed the knife until morning. The knife then was so damaged that it was not fine on the morrow. Coirpre then made a great complaint about it and was mournful and demanded justice for it from his friend. 'That is fair. I shall pay for that wrong', he said. 'I shall take nothing', said Coirpre, 'but what is in the law of the Britons: "every criminal for his crime"'. Thus the lap-dog was handed over for his crime, and the name, Mug Éime, was given to it.

The lap-dog was female and it was pregnant when she was taken over to Ireland. Ailill Fland Bec was king of Munster at that time and Cormac úa Conn held the kingship of Tara. They began immediately to seek and contend for the dog. And this was the arrangement they established between them: the dog should be for a fixed time in the house of each. The dog gave birth subsequently and each took a pup from its litter so that they name each one after her, and the men of Ireland divided them between them. And it is from that lap-dog that all the lap-dogs of Ireland descend, *so the Irish relate*.

Later the lap-dog died. A long time later Conla mac Tadg mac Cían mac Ailell Ólomm found the bare skull of that dog and put his question to the poet who had come with a poem for his father, i.e. Máon mac Étna was *the name of that poet*. The poet then solved it by means of *teinm laido*:

Fine the abundance in the house of Uí Eogain,
fat in the house of Uí Chind,
Let everyone heal your anger;
May you be fair in the house of Coirpre Músc, Mugéime.

That was the head of Mug Éime, the first lap-dog to be brought to Ireland.

Orc tréith (Y 1018 = *SC* O21)

Orc tréith 'son of a king' i.e. the name for the son of a king; for a king is called *tríath*. A fair of a king's son, i.e. food and valuable clothing, feathers and coverlets, draughts and chess, horses and chariots, hunting dogs and other pets besides.

Orc is a name for a salmon; thus the head of Lomna the fool spoke after it had been struck off, 'A speckled, white-breasted salmon which bursts with spawn under the seas. Not talkative, not silent is the chief of the people who does not get abundance. You made a division which is not right, Coirpre'.

That was as a result of the following: Finn úa Baiscni had as a fool Lomna Midlach. Finn went out one day on a hunting trip. Lomna remained behind. Finn had a woman of the Luigne; for indeed in every mountain region and every forest that Finn used to frequent with his warrior band, there used to be a particular woman waiting for him in the nearest inhabited land. These were female hospitallers and they were good at supporting the warrior bands, for their reputation would spread out over the lands so that no-one would dare to harm them. Find happened then to be in Tethba with his warrior band, and went on a hunting trip, and Lomna stayed behind. As he was wandering outside, he came upon Coirpre, a warrior, lying with Finn's woman in secret. The woman begged Lomna to conceal it, but betraying Finn troubled him. Finn arrived then. Lomna cut an ogam then on a four-sided rod, and this was what was on it: 'A wooden stake on a fence of silver; hellebore among the water-cress; the husband of a wanton woman is foolish according to the learned Féni. It is heather on bare Úalann of the Luigne'.

Finn understood the message and was disgusted with the woman. The woman, however, realized that it had been discovered through Lomna, and a message went from her to Coirpre and he came and killed the fool, and took his head off and took it with him. Finn came to the bothy at the end of the day and came across the headless corpse. 'That is a body without a head', said Finn. 'Let it be discovered for us', said the warrior band, 'whose the body is'. Then Finn put his thumb into his mouth and prophezied through *teinm laodae* and said, 'He does not slay people; he does not chop (them) down; he did not strike (them) down with death; he does not redden (them); he does not slay a boar; he does not redden (it); he cannot summon (it), and he has not brought (it) into the grave, namely, he Lomnae. This is the body of Lomna', said Finn, 'and enemies have taken his head from him'.[70]

They fetched their hounds and set them on the track of the young men and found them in an empty house cooking a fish on a griddle and the head of Lomna was on a stake by the fire. The first helping taken from the griddle Coirpre shared between the three nines and not even a morsel was put into the mouth of the head then. It was prohibition for Finn. It was then the head said to them, 'A speckled, white-breasted salmon which bursts with spawn under the seas', i.e. a salmon from spawn, 'that is its substance'.

The second helping taken from the fire or the griddle Coirpre divided *again in the same way as before*, and the head was heard to say, 'You have divided the share at the second re-division, a division of a second cutting, according to intoxicating smoke (?). It would be fitting that a portion for my belly be given soon. There will be a leader of a warrior-band with you, Luigni'. 'Put the head away, as it is saying bad words to us', said Coirpre. And the head was heard from a distance, 'A deceptive host have vanquished me in a swift rush of the slaughter of battle. I felt confusion. The hour of my death was of no consequence to you, but it may be that my killing will cause suffering. A fire lit by Finn by which the Luigni will blaze'.[71]

With that, Finn came and killed him.

Prull (Y 1059 = *SC* P19)
Prull 'greatly', increase and augmentation, as the female-poet, daughter of úa Dulsaine, said to Senchán Torpéist in the Isle of Man, i.e.

'my two ears burn me greatly'.

Then the apprentice poet of the retinue of Senchán replied, i.e.

'the poet, child of úa Dulsaine,
from Lia Toll Taursaige'.

70 Note that the translation of this prophecy is extremely problematic. **71** Again note that the translation of this utterance is extremely problematic.

This is how that happened to Senchán. He happened to go on a journey to the Isle of Man, i.e. a pleasure trip to make a circuit there. Fifty poets was their number, not including apprentice-poets. Hardly any poet before that had worn the like of Senchán's clothing, not to mention his sage's mantle, etc. What was best of the clothing of a noble of the Irishmen, that is what the poets wore.

When, however, that put out to sea and set the stern towards land, a lad of unnatural appearance addressed them from the shore: 'Let me go with you!', he said. They all look at the lad. They did not wish to let him join them, for they thought that he was not a bird fit for their flock because his appearance was hideous. To begin with, when someone would put their finger on his brow, a spurt of putrid matter would pour down the back of his neck. He had a rough caul over the crown of his head as far as the cartilage of his two shoulder-blades.[72] Anyone who saw it would think that clots of his brain had broken through his skull. His two eyes were as bulbous as a blackbird's egg, as swift as a (?), as black as death. The points of his teeth were as yellow as gold, their bases as green as a holly-trunk. Two bare, skinny legs, two pointy dark-speckled heels beneath him. If the rag he wore were stripped off him, it would not be difficult for it to move by itself, unless a stone were put on it, on account of the number of its vermin.

He shouted loudly to Senchán and said to him, 'I shall be of greater use to you than the arrogant, foolish crowd that is around you'. 'Can you come along the rudder into the boat?' 'I shall try', he said. He stepped then along the rudder into the boat, as swiftly as a mouse along a loom-beam, until he was in the boat. The boat with its load almost sank, since the poets pressed forward away from him from one end of the vessel to the other, and they said as if with one voice, 'A monster has reached you, Senchán; it will be your only retinue, if only we could escape to land'. It is on account of that that Senchán Torpéist [< *do·rorban* 'reach' + *péist* 'monster'], i.e. Senchán whom the monster reached.

They reached the Isle of Man after that. They brought their boat ashore. When they were going along the shore, they saw the tall, grey-haired old woman on a rock, *as the poet said*:[73]

> An old woman and an old churl,
> Their decrepit beard was a grave broom,
> provided (?) that they do not serve the son of God
> and they do not give their first-fruits

72 The B version has a much longer description in place of the next four sentences, which is given at the end of the story. **73** The poem is omitted in La and M.

In this way was the old woman on the shore reaping seaweed and other sea-produce besides. Excellent and noble were her feet and hands, but the clothing she wore was not fine and the emaciation of famine was upon her, and that was pitiful, for she was the female-poet, the daughter of úa Dulsaine from Múscraige of Lia Toll from the territory of Uí Fhidgenti. She had gone on a circuit of Ireland and Britain and Man, and all her retinue were dead. Her brother, the son of úa Dulsaine, a fine poet also, was searching for her through the territories of Ireland and did not find her etc.

When the old woman saw the poets, she asked who they were. One of them then said, 'The one who askes this is not from his land; this is Senchán, poet of all Ireland'.

> 'Do you have enough humility', she said, 'to wait and hear what I have to say?'
> 'I do, indeed', said Senchán.
> '"I was not accustomed to knotty tribulation,
> although I reap blistered seaweed."
> What is its other half-stanza?'

Senchán grows silent then, as do all the poets. Then the aforementioned lad leaps out in front of Senchán and said, 'Silent, woman! Do not address Senchán! It is not fitting for you. Address me in this way, since no other from this retinue will address you'.

> 'If that is so', said the female-poet, 'what is its other half-quatrain?'
> 'Not difficult', he said:
> '"From the top of a rock in the sea of Man
> much salt has been made here"'.
> 'True', she said, 'and now this half-quatrain:
> "My two ears burn me greatly".
> What is its other half-quatrain, Senchán?'
> 'What?', said the lad, 'are you still trying to address Senchán? He will not speak to you'.
> 'Well then, what do you think it is?'
> 'Not difficult', he said:
> '"The poet, child of úa Dulsaine
> from Lia Toll Taursaige"'.
> 'That is true' said Senchán, 'Are you the daughter of úa Dulsaine, the female poet who is being sought throughout Ireland?'
> 'I am indeed', she said. Then she was bathed by Senchán then. She was given beautiful clothing and she came with Senchán to Ireland.

When Senchán came to Ireland they saw the aforementioned lad. For he was now a radiant, kingly youth, very tall, large-eyed, very martial, with a gold-yellow head of hair, tied with gold thread and dressed in tresses, as curly as the pegs of a harp; he had very fine, regal clothing, a golden brooch binding that clothing. A purple, bossed four-edged shield on his left arm, covered with gems, carbuncles and valuable stones and pearls and crystal and sapphires. A straight-bladed sword with incantations of red-gold on its discs; a noble diadem with a golden crown on his head. The finest appearance and greatest brightness which was ever upon a man was upon him.

He then came right-hand wise around Senchán and his retinue, *and he has appeared nowhere since that time. And there is no doubt that he was the spirit of Poetry*.

In place of
Anyone who saw it would think that clots of his brain ... two pointy dark-speckled heels beneath him (p. 41).

The B version has
The dripping of his brain which had been poured (?) over his ears was like a continual stream. As for the join of his head and his skull, it did not cease from gushing out stench. His two eyes were as bulbous as a blackbird's egg; his glance as swift as a millstone, his face as black as death, his two cheeks more bulbous than a lifting-crane. His nose was as long as the spout of a smith's bellows. Like the blowing of bellows smelting ore was the inhaling and exhaling of his breath. Hammers would not strike from a red-hot mass of metal what his lips would strike forth of fire. He was as swift as a swallow or a hare over the ground. The tips of his teeth were as yellow as gold, the base as green as holly. His two shins bare and thin, covered in spots, beneath him; his two heels spiked, yellow with dark spots; his shin like a distaff, his thigh like an axe-handle; his buttock like a half-cheese; his belly like a bushel-sack; his throat like the neck of a heron; his head the size of the massive round head of a soldier; his hands as long as pitch-forks; his fists as big as the fists of a slave.

ABBREVIATIONS

Sanas Cormaic (SC)

B — Leabhar Breac (Dublin, Royal Irish Academy, MS 23 P 16), pp 263–72 = W. Stokes (ed.), *Three Irish glossaries* (London: Williams & Norgate, 1862 (rpr Felinfach: Llanerch, 2000)), pp 1–44 = J. O'Donovan and W. Stokes (trans. and eds), *Cormac's glossary* (Calcutta, Irish Archaeological and Celtic

Society, 1868) (= Stokes's version *A*) [reference by page and line number of Stokes's edition].

H[1a] TCD, MS 1317 (H.2.15[b]), pp 13–37 (= Stokes's version C).

H[1b] TCD, MS 1317 (H.2.15[b]), pp 77–102 (= Stokes's version C).

L The Book of Leinster (T.C.D., MS 1339 (H.2.18), p. 179 = R. I. Best, M.A. O'Brien (eds), *Book of Leinster*, iv (Dublin: Dublin Institute for Advanced Studies, 1965), pp 780–1 = Stokes, *Three Irish glossaries*, pp 44–5 (incomplete = Y 1224–34 (T) and Y 1268–75 (U) = Stokes's version F) [reference by the line numbers in Best and O'Brien's diplomatic edition].

La Oxford, Bodleian Library, MS Laud 610, fols 79[r]–84[r] = W. Stokes (ed. and trans.), 'On the Bodleian fragment of Cormac's Glossary', *Transactions of the Philological Society*, 1901, pp 149–206 (incomplete = Y 756–1224 (*I–T*) = Stokes's version G) [reference by the numbering of items in Stokes's edition].

M The Book of Uí Maine (Dublin, RIA, MS D.ii.1), pp 177–84[a] = K. Meyer (ed.), 'Cormacs Glossar nach der Handschrift des Buches der Uí Maine', *Sitzungsberichte der preussischen Akademie der Wissenschaften zu Berlin*, Phil.-hist. Kl., 1919, pp 290–321 (incomplete; only up to Y 1224) [reference by the numbering according to Y].

Y The Yellow Book of Lecan (TCD, MS 1318 (H.2.16)), pp 255[a]–83[a] = K. Meyer (ed.), '*Sanas Cormaic*', *Anecdota from Irish manuscripts*, iv (Halle: Niemeyer, 1912; reprinted with Meyer's corrections added to the text, Felinfach: Llanerch, 1994) = O'Donovan and Stokes, *Cormac's glossary* (especially for YAdd) (= Stokes's version B) [reference by the numbering of items in Meyer's edition].

YAdd The additional material in Y, H[1a] and H[1b], not found in the other versions of the glossary [reference by the numbering of items in Meyer's edition].

Other abbreviations

CIH D.A. Binchy (ed.), *Corpus iuris Hibernici*, 6 vols (Dublin: DIAS, 1978).

DDC *Dúil Dromma Cetta*; the fullest version is *D*[1] preserved in Dublin, Trinity College, MS 1337 (H.3.18), pp 63–75 = *CIH* ii, 604.39–622.12 = W. Stokes (ed.), 'Irish glosses', *Transactions of the Philological Society*, 1859, pp 170–97 (partially = Meyer's *H*[2] (*Anecdota* iv, viii)) [reference by page and line number to the *CIH* text].

DIL E.G. Quin et al. (*Contributions to a*) *Dictionary of the Irish language based mainly on Old and Middle Irish materials* (Dublin: Royal Irish Academy, 1913–76; compact edition: Dublin: Royal Irish Academy, 1990); an electronically searchable version is now on-line at http://www.dil.ie/.

O'Dav O'Davoren's Glossary; the fullest version is *ODav1* preserved in London, BL, MS Egerton 88, fols. 79[a]–92[c] = *CIH* iv 1466.11–1531.24 = W. Stokes (ed.), 'O'Davoren's glossary', *Archiv für celtische Lexicographie* 2 (1904), pp

197–504 (text partially emended by reference to *O'Dav*^{2}) = Stokes, *Three Irish glossaries*, pp 47–124 (text based solely on *ODav*^{1}) [reference by the numbering of items in Stokes's *Archiv* edition].

OM O'Mulconry's Glossary; the fullest version is *OM*^{1} preserved in The Yellow Book of Lecan (T.C.D., MS 1318 (H.2.16)), cols 88–122 = W. Stokes (ed.), 'O'Mulconry's glossary', *Archiv für celtische Lexicographie* 1 (1900), pp 232–324 [references by the numbering of items in Stokes's edition].

SC *Sanas Cormaic* (see above).

The Assassination of Diarmait mac Cerbaill

MICHAEL MECKLER

Diarmait mac Cerbaill was for two decades the high-king of the Ui Néill kindred, holding the ceremonial site of Tara during one of the most important periods in early Irish history. Based on the Annals of Ulster, Diarmait's reign has been calculated to have lasted from the year 544 to his death in 565.[1]

In the middle of the sixth century, Ireland truly emerges into the historical record. The plague that ravages the reconquered Mediterranean empire of Justinian also sweeps through Ireland *(AU* 553). Holy men are busily establishing monasteries: Kieran founds Clonmacnoise *(AU* 547), Comgall founds Bangor *(AU* 554), Brendan founds Clonfert *(AU* 557) and Columba founds Iona *(AU* 562). And the ancient gathering called the Feast of Tara may well have been celebrated for the final time *(AU* 557).[2]

Diarmait's long reign would loom large in the Irish historical consciousness. Throughout the Middle Ages, when the Irish felt compelled to refashion their models of political, religious and social organization, they hearkened back to Diarmait's reign, elaborating upon traditions about Diarmait to provide interpretations and reflections of contemporary concerns. Irish legends, Irish and Latin hagiography, and annalistic entries dealing with Diarmait's death provide examples of the uses to which early Irish history was employed.

Francis Byrne once noted that 'nothing in Diarmait's life became him like the leaving it.'[3] The sparse annalistic tradition states that Diarmait was murdered. Byrne, however, had in mind the wonderful *aided* 'death tale'

1 Second and subsequent references to medieval Irish annals will use the following abbreviations: *ATig* = Whitley Stokes (ed.), 'The Annals of Tigernach, third fragment', *Revue celtique* 17 (1896), 119–263; *AI* = Sean Mac Airt (ed.), *The Annals of Inisfallen* (Dublin: DIAS, 1951); *AU* = Sean Mac Airt and Gearóid Mac Niocaill (eds), *The Annals of Ulster (to A.D. 1131)* (Dublin: DIAS, 1983); *CS* = William M. Hennessy (ed.), *Chronicum Scotorum* (London: Longmans, Green, Reader, and Dyer, 1866). 2 D.A. Binchy, 'Fair of Tailtiu and the Feast of Tara', *Ériu* 18 (1958), 113–38; cf. Colmán Etchingham, 'Early medieval Irish history' in Kim McCone and Katharine Simms (eds), *Progress in medieval Irish studies* (Maynooth: Department of Old Irish, Saint Patrick's College, 1996), pp 123–53, esp. 131–3. 3 Francis John Byrne, *Irish kings and high-kings* (2nd ed., Dublin: Four Courts Press,

CSANA Yearbook 7: Four Courts Press, Dublin; ISSN 1649–0096; ISBN 978–1–84682–099–1

concerning Diarmait. This *aided* has come down to us in many places: parts of the story appear in both the Irish and Latin lives of saint Ruadán of Lorrha, as well as in the Irish life of Brendan of Clonfert; versions are found in the Book of Fermoy, the Book of Lismore, the Book of Uí Maine, the Yellow Book of Lecan and in British Library MS Egerton 1782.[4]

A summary of the tale (which does the beauty of the story no justice) runs like this: Diarmait has violated the sanctuary offered by Ruadán to Áed Guaire, who had previously killed Diarmait's herald after the herald told Áed Guaire to tear down the gate in front of Áed's house. Ruadán then gathers several holy men together and they march down to Tara, where the saints and Diarmait engage in a year of competitive fasting. Diarmait is tricked into eating and so begins negotiations to end the standoff. This leads to a few rounds of competitive cursing on the part of Diarmait and Ruadán, in which Ruadán portends the destruction of Tara, as well as the destruction of Diarmait, whose death is specifically said to be caused by the ridge-beam of his house falling on top of him. Diarmait dutifully has the ridge-beam removed and cast out into the sea. Meanwhile, a deal is worked out whereby Ruadán gets to take Áed Guaire home, and in exchange Diarmait gets some magical horses (which run away not too long after the deal has been finalized).

Diarmait now starts to get worried about his future and so consults his right-hand prophet Bec mac Dé. Bec mac Dé tells the king that he will be killed by the Ulster prince Áed the Black, who happens to be growing up in Diarmait's home after Diarmait had killed Áed's father. Áed the Black is then exiled to Britain. Diarmait also learns that he will be killed while wearing a shirt woven from flax grown from a single seed, drinking ale brewed from a single grain, and eating bacon from a pig that was not born. The king considers each of these occurrences so unlikely individually (let alone in tandem) that he continues not to think twice about eating pork, drinking beer and wearing linen. The king also discovers that he will die by slaying, by drowning and by burning, a combination also considered unlikely. (Experienced readers may already have an idea of where this tale is going.)

While on his travels through Ireland, Diarmait ends up a guest in the house of a mysterious Banbán, and there Diarmait puts on a linen shirt,

2001), p. 97. 4 Johan Corthals, *Manuscript sources to Old and Middle Irish tales (MS-OMIT)*, February 2007 edition, website, http://www.ucc.ie/celt/MS-OMIT/index.htm [viewed 1 July 2007]. The versions in the Book of Lismore and MS Egerton 1782 were edited and translated by Standish H. O'Grady, *Silva Gadelica* (London: Williams and Norgate, 1892), vol. 1, pp 66–82 (edition); vol. 2, pp 70–88 (translation). John Carey provided a partial translation based on O'Grady's edition in John T. Koch (ed.), *The Celtic heroic age* (3rd ed., Andover, MA: Celtic Studies Publications, 2000), pp 200–4. Dan M. Wiley edited the text from the Book of Uí Maine with variants from the Yellow Book of Lecan and MS Egerton 1782 in his 2000 Harvard PhD dissertation, and he provided a translation of the Book of Lismore version in 'Stories about Diarmait mac Cerbaill from the Book of Lismore',

drinks some ale and eats some bacon. The king's host reveals that through the wonders of agriculture combined with heritage seed preservation, the flax for the shirt and the grain for the ale each go back generations to a single seed. Banbán also reveals advances in animal husbandry by telling the king that his piglets are brought into the world by Caesarian section rather than natural delivery. Diarmait then notices that the ridge-beam of the house looks different from the rest of the carpentry. His host tells the king that the beam was found floating in the sea by some fishermen and Banbán had it incorporated into his house.

Diarmait is now seized with the realization that things do not look good. He tries to rush out of the house but there to meet him in the doorway is – as one might guess – Áed the Black. Áed the Black transfixes Diarmait with a spear. Diarmait staggers back into the house, which is set on fire. The king ends up drowning in the ale-vat, and finally the ridge-beam falls on top of him. End of Diarmait, whose head gets taken to Clonmacnoise for burial, and end of story.

Áed's motivation for assassinating Diarmait is never made explicit, though two reasons for revenge are available: Diarmait's killing of Áed's father, and Áed's abrupt exile at Diarmait's command. The *Aided Diarmata* is not concerned with Áed's motivation because Áed is portrayed as an agent of the king's destruction, an agent operating merely as a part of divine will.

The *Aided Diarmata* has been discussed by several scholars, including Joan Radner. She saw the tale, which is among the most complex elaborations of the threefold-death motif in Irish literature, as a plea for cooperation and compromise between religious and secular authorities. The preoccupation with sanctuary rights echoes concerns among the clergy in the eleventh century, and Radner made a strong argument for dating the composition of the tale to shortly after 1022. The more elaborate versions, which contain an introductory passage on Diarmait's support of Kieran in the foundation of Clonmacnoise and a conclusion that mentions Diarmait's head being buried at Clonmacnoise, point to the monastery as the place of its composition.[5] Another late but much sparser tradition shows Diarmait as a Lear figure who lost control of his realm as the indirect result of disputes with various clergymen. Diarmait seeks repentence and prays for an early death. Both the repentence and the request find divine favor, but in this tradition no details about the death are provided.[6]

Emania 19 (2002), 53–9. **5** Joan Newlon Radner, 'The significance of the threefold death in Celtic tradition' in Patrick K. Ford (ed.), *Celtic folklore and Christianity* (Santa Barbara: McNally and Loftin, 1983), pp 180–99. Richard Sharpe, *Medieval Irish saints' lives* (Oxford: Oxford University Press, 1991), p. 332, understands the version transmitted in the Latin life of Ruadán as an addition to the original text, an addition that had been translated into Latin perhaps as late as the fourteenth century. **6** This tradition underlies the quatrain that begins 'Tri ní do ben dím mo rath' in A.

Adomnán's *Life of Columba,* written but a century and a quarter after Diarmait's death, mentions the king's murder in an episode that itself concerns a threefold death, but not that of Diarmait – rather, that of Áed the Black. Sometime after the murder, Áed was brought in clerical garb to Tiree by a priest named Findchán, who kept Áed at his monastery called Artchain. Findchán arranged for Áed to be ordained a priest himself, and a bishop was brought in for the purpose. The bishop, however, was said to be reluctant, and during the ceremony did not lay his hand upon Áed's head until Findchán did so first. When Columba heard about this, the saint was not pleased, predicting that Findchán's hand would rot and fall off. Columba also announced that Áed would return to his bloody ways like a dog to its vomit, and that he would be killed by being struck by a spear, falling from a boat and drowning in water. Columba is said to have added that Áed deserved to die even sooner for murdering the king of all Ireland. Adomnán then reveals that the events took place as predicted.[7]

The passage is of special interest with regard to the development of the concept of high-kingship. Diarmait is described by Adomnán, and in Columba's own words as relayed by Adomnán, as the 'king of all Ireland' (*totius Scotiae regnatorem; totius regem … Scotiae*). Moreover, Diarmait is described as having been a ruler 'ordained by God's authority' (*deo auctore ordinatum*). These phrases show that even by the end of the seventh century, when Adomnán was writing, the concept of the high-kingship was already in bloom. As high-king, Diarmait was viewed on seventh-century Iona as holding a divine mandate. The breaking of that mandate through assassination was posited as an attack on God's ordering of the world.[8]

An obvious question related to Adomnán's story of Áed the Black is whether Áed's stay on Tiree was connected with the assassination. Richard Sharpe, in his translation of Adomnán, assumed not, relating the visit to internal disputes among the Ulaid.[9] The wording of the passage, while identifying Áed as Diarmait's murderer, does not specifically call the visit a result of the assassination, even though the assassination seems to be the cause of Columba's hostility towards Áed. Áed's career between the murder of Diarmait mac Cerbaill *c.*565 and Áed's elevation as king of the Ulaid *c.*581 is unknown apart from this episode.

The Ulaid had an unusual political structure. There were two distinct ethnic groups – the Cruthin and the Érainn – and kingship over this 'Fifth' of Ireland switched between the two, with kings from the dominant Dál

O'Kelleher and G. Schoepperle (eds), *Betha Colaim Chille compiled by Manus O'Donnell* (Urbana: University of Illinois, 1918), ch. 139, p. 140. **7** Adomnán, *Vita Columbae* 1.36. **8** Byrne, *Irish kings,* pp 96–7; Richard Sharpe (trans.), *Adomnán of Iona, Life of St Columba* (London: Penguin, 1995), pp 296–7. **9** Sharpe, *Columba,* pp 297–8.

Fiatach kindred from the Érainn alternating with Cruthin kings, usually from the Dál nAraidi kindred. Áed the Black was a prince of the Dál nAraidi.[10]

When Diarmait was killed, Demmán mac Cairill of the Dál Fiatach was the Ulster king. Demmán became king by defeating and killing the previous king, a distant kinsman, at a battle dated to 557 *(ATig, CS* 557; *AU* 556). Demmán would himself be killed by shepherds roughly a decade later at a location identified as being near the modern town of Dromara in Co. Down *(ATig, CS* 568; *AU* 571).[11] This area would have been populated by Cruthin, but not those of the Dál nAraidi kindred but rather from the seemingly unrelated Uí Echach Cobo kindred.[12]

Demmán was succeeded by his brother Báetán. Báetán seems to have been an ambitious and energetic leader who attempted to extend his authority to the Isle of Man and possibly to Galloway.[13] Pressure was certainly felt by the Dál Riata of Argyll, who maintained a tenuous hold on ancestral lands in the very northern tip of Ulster and whose king, Áedan mac Gabráin, is reported in the sources to have been engaged in conflict with Báetán, and to have submitted to him.[14] Áed the Black would certainly have been seen as a potential rival for the Ulster kingship, and he in fact succeeded Báetán after Báetán died a natural death *c.*581 *(AU* 580). For the Dál Riata, the possibility of causing dissention among the Ulaid by having a potential king nearby may have seemed advantageous, though it should be kept in mind that Áed was being sheltered at a monastery on Tiree and not at the court of the Dál Riata king.[15] Findchán, like the far more famous Comgall of Bangor (whose Latin life claims that Comgall, too, founded a short-lived monastery on Tiree), was an Ulsterman who belonged to the Dál nAraidi, so whatever the direct cause may have been for Áed's banishment from Ulster, his stay on Tiree reflected the support Áed had among his kinsmen.[16]

The final set of texts providing information on Diarmait's assassination are the Irish annals. During the past half century, a great deal of work has been done trying to untangle the sources and relationships among the

10 On the Ulaid in this period, see Dáibhí Ó Cróinín, *Early medieval Ireland, 400–1200* (London: Longman, 1995), pp 48–52; T.M. Charles-Edwards, *Early Christian Ireland* (Cambridge: Cambridge University Press, 2000), pp 54–67. **11** Edmund Hogan, *Onomasticon Goedelicum* (Dublin: Four Courts Press, 1993), p. 118 (*boirenn*). **12** Byrne, *Irish kings,* p. 109. **13** Ó Cróinín, *Early medieval Ireland,* pp 50–1. **14** Michael Meckler, 'Colum Cille's ordination of Áedán mac Gabráin', *Innes Review* 41 (1990), 139–50; the famous meeting at Druim Cett involving Áedán was not, however, connected to Báetán's activities; see Sharpe, *Columba,* p. 313. Sharpe's arguments are not convincingly refuted by Bart Jaski, 'Druim Cett revisited', *Peritia* 12 (1998), 340–50. **15** On other examples of Dál Riata conflict with their Ulster neighbors, see Charles-Edwards, *Early Christian Ireland,* pp 59–61. **16** Michael Meckler, 'Carnal love and priestly ordination on sixth-century Tiree', *Innes review* 51 (2000), 95–108. On Comgall and Tiree, see *Vita Sancti Comgalli*, ch. 22, in Charles Plummer (ed.), *Vitae sanctorum Hiberniae* (Oxford: Clarendon Press, 1910), vol. 2, p. 11.

various annals.[17] This work has shown that for the period before the year 912, where the Annals of Ulster and the Annals of Tigernach have similar entries, those entries were part of an earlier work that has been dubbed the 'Chronicle of Ireland'. This 'Chronicle of Ireland' was itself based on an earlier chronicle kept at Iona beginning *c.*680 and continuing until *c.*740. This 'Iona Chronicle' was written in Latin, and the date of its origin corresponds to the abbacy of Adomnán (679–704), whose investigations are probably responsible for many of the earlier Latin entries on Irish and Scottish matters, especially those involving his own Uí Néill kindred. Annal entries written in Irish postdate the 'Iona Chronicle' by at least seventy years, and so the appearance of pre-ninth-century information in Irish represents the interpolation of later material. The Annals of Inisfallen are also useful as check on *ATig.* Similar entries seem to reveal a common source up to *c.*1065, and that common source seems to have been composed at Clonmacnoise. This common source also appears to underlie the *Chronicum Scotorum.*[18]

In recent years, examinations of the kalends-and-ferial dating system that appears in some of the annals has somewhat muddied the picture. The kalends-and-ferial system – identifying the year by indicating the day of the week on which 1 January fell on that particular year – has been shown to have been related to how the Irish calculated the date of Easter through the early eighth century.[19] The system as it currently appears in manuscripts of various annals is horribly corrupt, though the corruptions can be rationalized. Since rationalization is more easily carried out on *ATig* and *CS* than on *AU,* it was argued that the dating of events in *AU* – where the more familiar *anno Domini* dating system was probably calculated in the tenth century for the entries going back to the year 431, and then added onto the annals collection that later became *AU* – was less reliable than the kalends-and-ferial dating in the Clonmacnoise tradition from which *ATig* and *CS* derive.[20]

17 See, most notably, John Bannerman, 'Notes on the Scottish entries in the early Irish annals', in *Studies in the history of Dalriada* (Edinburgh: Scottish Academic Press, 1974), pp 9–26 [originally in *Scottish Gaelic studies* 11 (1968), 149–70]; Kathleen Hughes, *Early Christian Ireland: introduction to the sources* (London: Hodder and Stoughton, 1972), pp 97–159; Geróid Mac Niocaill, *The medieval Irish annals* (Dublin: Dublin Historical Association, 1975); Kathryn Grabowski and David Dumville, *Chronicles and annals of medieval Ireland and Wales* (Woodbridge: Boydell Press, 1984); Michael Meckler, 'The *Annals of Ulster* and the date of the meeting at Druim Cett', *Peritia* 11 (1997), pp 44–52. **18** See n. 1 for editions. **19** Dáibhí Ó Cróinín, 'Early Irish annals from Easter tables: a case restated', *Peritia* 2 (1983), 74–86; Daniel P. McCarthy and Dáibhí Ó Cróinín, 'The "lost" Irish 84-year Easter table rediscovered', *Peritia* 6–7 (1987–8), 227–42. **20** Daniel P. McCarthy, 'The chronology of the Irish annals', *Proceedings of the Royal Irish Academy* 98C (1988), 203–55; McCarthy, 'The chronological apparatus of the *Annals of Ulster* ad 431–1131', *Peritia* 8 (1994), 46–79, provided an overly convoluted process for the imposition of *anno Domini* dating. Nonetheless, his assertion seems valid that the bulk of *anno Domini* dating in what became *AU* must have initially been

Certainly sometime in the twelfth century, the chronological ordering of the earlier entries in what became *AU* was heavily scrutinized, with additions made in what had been empty years in the 'Chronicle of Ireland' and the proposed redating of certain events.[21] This work, which was carried out either in Armagh or Derry, reflected serious concern with the reliability of the 'Chronicle of Ireland' dates for pre-ninth-century events. So in the twelfth century, the chronology better represented today by *ATig* and *CS* came under question. While some twenty-first-century scholars seem far less troubled than their twelfth-century predecessors about the reliability of *ATig* and *CS* dates, nonetheless the modern source criticism carried out on the *content* of the individual entries – positing an 'Iona Chronicle' initially composed *c.* 680, and a ninth-century 'Chronicle of Ireland' which ended in 912 – maintains wide scholarly acceptance.[22]

A comparison of Diarmait mac Cerbaill's death notices in *AU* 564 and *ATig* readily demonstrates what must have been the entry in the 'Iona Chronicle', namely something extremely close to the *AU* entry: *Occisio Diarmato m Cerbuill cui successerunt duo filii Mc Erce, Forgus 7 Domnall.*[23] No mention is made of who killed Diarmait or where the murder took place.

ATig and *AI* provide this information. The *AI* entry corresponding to the year 564 reads: *Mors Diarmata m. Cerbaill quem interfecit Áed Dub i rRáith Bicc.* This entry itself seems to have three sources. The phrase *Mors Diarmata m. Cerbaill* is ultimately based on the 'Iona Chronicle' entry (via the 'Chronicle of Ireland'); the phrase *quem interfecit Áed Dub* is quite close to language used by Adomnán in the *Life of Columba* 1.36: *Qui (= Aidus Niger) et Diormitium filium Cerbulis … interficerat,* which may well be the ultimate source, though perhaps one should not make too much of this; finally, the Irish phrase *i rRáith Bicc,* giving a location, is also found in *ATig* immediately after the Latin information *(Diarmuit mac Cerbaill occisus est)* based ultimately on the 'Iona Chronicle', indicating a common source. When this additional information – *i rRaith Bicc* – was added at Clonmacnoise is difficult to

devised sometime between 890 and 1014. **21** Meckler, 'Annals of Ulster', 47–52. The imposition into *AU* of notices from a *Book of Dub dá Leithe,* which must refer to the mid-eleventh-century Armagh cleric (died 1064); and from a *Book of Cuanu,* whose author has been identified by Daniel McCarthy, 'The chronological apparatus of the Annals of Ulster AD 82–1019', *Peritia* 16 (2002), 256–83, esp. 279–81, with a Cuan hua Lothcháin killed in 1024; along with McCarthy's argument, that the chronological apparatus in what became *AU* was revised based on a work written *c.*1020 – all support the idea that dissatisfaction with the 'Chronicle of Ireland' chronology led to the consultation of multiple sources when what became *AU* was substantially revised in the twelfth century. **22** Even Daniel McCarthy, 'The original compilation of the Annals of Ulster', *Studia Celtica* 38 (2004), 69–95, accepts the primacy of the language and content of *AU*'s entries, even though he prefers the Clonmacnoise dating for the corresponding events. **23** The final words, *Forgus 7 Domnall,* which seem like a supplement, may not have been in the 'Iona Chronicle', but were certainly included in the 'Chronicle of Ireland'.

pinpoint, but it must have been between 912 (after the 'Chronicle of Ireland' was complete) and 1065 (when *AI* no longer contains entries similar enough to *ATig* to reveal a common source). In other words, the location of Ráth Bec for the assassination of Diarmait mac Cerbaill was not supplied in the annals until the tenth century at the earliest, and quite possibly the eleventh. If we now take note of the proposed composition date of *Aided Diarmata* of shortly after 1022, it seems quite likely the *Aided* became the source for this addition to the chronicles giving the location of Diarmait's assassination.[24]

There is additional evidence of interest in this regard. *ATig* further define the location as *a Muig Line* 'of the Plain of Line', which corresponds to the region near Antrim town in modern Co. Antrim. This further identification might have been deemed necessary because *Ráth Bec,* which means 'small fort', was not an uncommon placename, and Hogan's *Onomasticon Goedelicum* lists eight sites with forms of the name.[25] The Book of Lismore version of the *Aided Diarmata* names Ráth Bec as the site of the assassination, but without further locating the site. The version in ms. Egerton 1782 also mentions Ráth Bec, but this version explicitly locates the site in Ulster. In ms. Egerton 1782, Diarmait is said to be taking part in the annual circuit of the high-king that began in Leinster and moved clockwise to end in Ulster, and that the Ulstermen surrounded Banbán's home to prevent Diarmait from escaping the burning dwelling.[26] A more direct connection between *ATig* and the version of the *Aided Diarmata* in ms. Egerton 1782 is the notice that Diarmait's head was later buried at Clonmacnoise. The detail of the body being buried at Connor in Co. Antrim, a detail *not* found in any version of the *Aided Diarmata,* appears only in post-*AI* annals of the Clonmacnoise group, such as *CS.*[27]

Thomas Charles-Edwards claimed that Columba's hostility towards Áed the Black stemmed from Áed's killing of Diarmait while the Ulsterman was offering the high-king hospitality.[28] Adomnán's text, however, does not give this as the reason – and indeed provides a *different* reason involving the divine

24 Charles-Edwards, *Early Christian Ireland,* p. 527 n. 21, asserts that the identification of Ráth Bec as the assassination site 'may well have been in the Chronicle of Ireland and in its source, the Iona annals,' but the application of source-criticism methodology to the relevant entries in *ATig* and *AI* makes his assertion unlikely; see the references listed in n. 17 for how this methodology was derived. **25** Hogan, *Onomasticon,* p. 567. **26** O'Grady, *Silva Gadelica* 1.80–2: 'Luid Diarmait iar sin for a cuairt rígi deissil Erenn. ár iss amlaid no caithedh rí Temrach Erinn .i. a Temraig i lLaighnib ocus a sidéin a Mumain ocus a sin i Connachtaib ocus for cóicedh Ulad fó deoidh. contoirched co Temraig i gcoinn úidhe na bliadna forsin samfuin do fritháilim na samhna ocus fer nErenn im féiss Temrach. Dia mbái Diarmait laa nann forsinn cuairt sin confaco in laech cuice issintech. ... gabsat Ulaid amuig immon tech ocus loiscter iarum in tech forru'; Wiley, 'Stories about Diarmait', 57. **27** *ATig:* 'a chend co Cluain; *CS*: a cend co Cluáin muc Nois co ro adnacht innte, ocus ro hadhnacht a Colaind hi Condér' O'Grady, Silva Gadelica 1.82: dobretha iar sin a chend ocus a thaissi co cluain mac Nóis cor hadhnaicedh isin chlaoin ferta nó isin céiti.' **28** Charles-Edwards,

sanctioning of secular authority. Furthermore, the *Aided Diarmata* does not show Áed the Black hosting Diarmait, but rather the host is the mysterious Banbán. The circumstances of how the historical Áed killed the historical Diarmait are unknown, but there is no textual evidence to support the notion that the assassination occurred while Áed was providing the hospitality due from a client to his lord.

Perhaps something might be gleaned from *AU*'s use of the term *occisio.* Violent deaths seem generally to have been described with three terms in the 'Iona Chronicle' material in *AU: occisio, iugulatio* or, when mentioning a battle, the name of the victim is given in the nominative followed by *cecidit.*[29] Leaving the battles aside, for the period between the years 431 and 680 (that is, information from the time of Patrick's mission until the time around when the 'Iona Chronicle' became a contemporary listing of events), ten entries use *occisio* or forms of the verb *occidere,* while thirty-six entries have *iugulatio* or forms of the verb *iugulare.* Diarmait mac Cerbaill is the first person whose death is described as an *occisio,* the others being Ainmire mac Sétna *(AU* 568), the two Uí Muiredaigh (Báetán mac Muirchertaigh and Echaid mac Domnaill, *AU* 571*),* Báetán mac Ninnedo *(AU* 585), Cumascach mac Áedo *(AU* 596), Sechnusach mac Garbáin *(AU* 608), the family of Báetán (Ailill mac Báetáin and Máel Duín mac Fergusa mac Báetáin, *AU* 619), Suibne Menn mac Fiachna *(AU* 627), Conall mac Suibne *(AU* 634) and Dúnchad mac Ultáin *(AU* 676*).*

What is immediately striking about this list is that all but Dúnchad mac Ultáin belonged to the Uí Néill. (Dúnchad's *occisio* may help scholars to fix the point at which the 'Iona Chronicle' became a contemporary record.) Moreover, based on the traditional genealogies, nine of these eleven Uí Néill were within the *indfine* 'end-kindred' of an abbot of Iona – that is, nine had a common ancestor within six generations of direct male descent with an abbot at the monastery where the chronicle was composed from which this list has been extracted.[30] In Irish law, the *indfine* marked the furthest extent of those who shared certain rights and responsibilities from belonging to the

Early Christian Ireland, p. 295. **29** Brian Ó Cuív, 'The motif of the threefold death', *Éigse* 15 (1973), 145–50, briefly examined the terminology of violent death in the annalistic tradition. **30** Byrne, *Irish kings,* pp 280–3; cf. M.A. O'Brien (ed.), *Corpus genealogiarum Hiberniae,* vol. 1 (Dublin: DIAS, 1976), pp 163–7. Ailbhe MacShamhráin, '*Nebulae discutiuntur*? The emergence of Clann Cholmáin, sixth-eighth centuries' in Alfred P. Smyth (ed.), *Seanchas: studies in early and medieval Irish archaeology, history and literature* (Dublin: Four Courts Press, 2000), pp 83–97, suggests that Diarmait mac Cerbaill was Columba's first cousin, making the king and his descendants much more closely related to the abbots of Iona than the traditional genealogies attest. Although MacShamhráin's reconstruction of Uí Néill relations is highly speculative, it enhances the argument that *AU*'s use of *occisio* in entries dated to the sixth and seventh centuries reflects the perspective of the Cenél Conaill branch of the Uí Néill on the slayings.

TABLE 1 *Occisio* in the 'Iona Chronicle' material from the *Annals of Ulster* for years 564–634, and the relationships between abbots of Iona and slain Uí Néill leaders

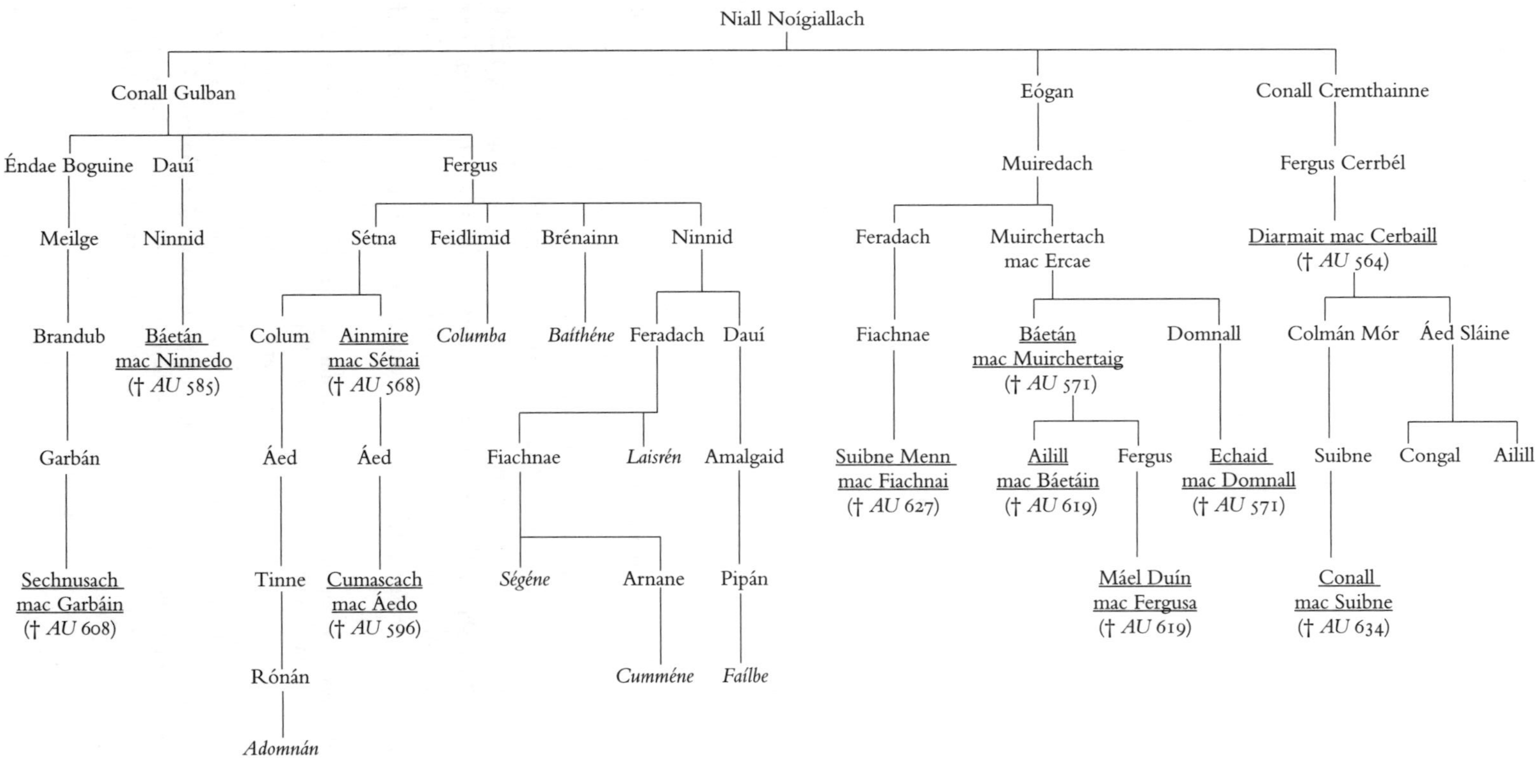

Those whose deaths are described with forms of the word *occisio* are underlined. Abbots of Iona are in *italics.*
(This chart follows the traditional genealogies as described by Francis John Byrne, *Irish kings and high-kings* (2nd ed., Dublin: Four Courts Press, 2001), pp 280–3; M.A. O'Brien (ed.), *Corpus genealogiarum Hiberniae,* vol. 1 (Dublin: Dublin Institute for Advanced Studies, 1976), pp 163–77.)

same kindred.[31] The murders of these Uí Néill leaders must have been particularly troubling to their kindred on Iona, and this may explain why the death notices are marked linguistically with the term *occisio* (fig. 1).

Further corroboration of this use of *occisio* in the 'Iona Chronicle' may be found in examining the notices of violent death for those responsible for *occisio.* Two, possibly three, such notices are known: for Áed the Black *(AU* 587); for Brandub mac Echach *(AU* 604), the murderer of Cumascach mac Áedo; and for Cumméne mac Colmáin *(AU* 627), if he is the same person named as a murderer forty-two years earlier of Báetán mac Ninnedo. Each of these three notices is described as *iugulatio.* Neither Áed the Black of the Ulaid nor Brandub of the Laigin belonged to the Uí Néill. Cumméne mac Colmáin, a grandson of Diarmait mac Cerbaill, was part of the Uí Néill, but he was at the very end of the *indfine* for the first three abbots of Iona, and *outside* the limits of kinship for subsequent Ui Néill abbots. Cumméne was also at the very end of the *indfine* for Báetán mac Ninnedo, the man he killed.[32]

The two *occisiones* of Ui Néill too distant to be reckoned an Iona abbot's kin are those of Máel Duín mac Fergusa (*AU* 619) and Conall mac Suibne (*AU* 634). Máel Duín mac Fergusa's killing took place with that of his uncle, Ailill mac Báetáin, who was in the *indfine.* Furthermore, the *AU* entry is introduced as *occisio geniris Baetain,* referring to Báetán mac Muirchertaig, Ailill's father, and Máel Duín's grandfather who was Columba's third cousin. Conall mac Suibne, a great-grandson of Diarmait mac Cerbaill, was involved in feuding between two branches of Diarmait's descendants: Clann Cholmáin (the branch to which Conall belonged), who became the kings of Mide; and the Síl nÁedo Sláine, who became the kings of Brega. Conall had killed two of his cousins the year before *(AU* 633), and those deaths were classified as *iugulationes.* When the brother of those cousins avenged the murders by killing Conall, that homicide was classified as *occisio.* Perhaps this classification represents Iona's opinion of the feud, which is paralleled by an episode in Adomnán's *Life of Columba* in which the saint issues a warning against kin-slaying to Áed Sláine, the son of Diarmait who founded the Brega dynasty.[33]

The difference between *iugulatio* and *occisio* may also reflect the distinction in Irish law between intentional homicides that could be classified as

31 On the *indfine* and the structure of Irish kinship, see Charles-Edward, *Kinship,* pp 23–165, esp. pp 44–61. Neil McLeod, 'Kinship', *Ériu* 51 (2000), 1–22, more narrowly defines the *indfine* as extending only through the great-grandchildren of a man's great-grandfather (second cousins) or the great-grandchildren of a man's grandfather (first cousins once removed), as opposed to fourth cousins. In McLeod's view, only Ainmire mac Sétnai and Báetán mac Ninnedo would have been reckoned within an Iona abbot's *indfine* based on the traditional genealogies. **32** In McLeod's interpretation of Irish kinship, Cumméne mac Colmáin was entirely outside the *indfine* of Iona abbots, as well as outside the *indfine* of Báetán mac Ninnedo. **33** Adommán, *Vita Columbae* 1.4; cf. Byrne, *Irish kings,* pp 96.

'forgivable slayings' (*gonai deithbiri*) and those that could not.[34] Exactly how the Irish legal concept manifests itself in these annalistic entries is hard to determine. The circumstances surrounding the killings mentioned in the annals may not be well enough known to allow modern scholars to fix direct correspondence between the Latin terminology of the annals and the Irish terminology of the law tracts. Furthermore, the 'Iona Chronicle' entries presumably represent the biases of the late seventh-century Cenél Conaill branch of the northern Uí Néill, the men who constituted the monastic institution's leadership.[35] Nonetheless, that a distinction between justifiable and non-justifiable homicide appears in both annals and law tracts suggests that the Latin terminology represents, in some way, an understanding of native law.

In any case, the varied sources dealing with the assassination of Diarmait mac Cerbaill demonstrate how meaningful the past was for the Irish when they needed to deal with important issues facing their society in the Middle Ages. Whether the issue involved what constituted justifiable homicide, or the religious and political foundations of kingship, or the proper function and respect of sanctuary rights, Diarmait's demise was called upon, and elaborated upon, to inform the matter.

34 Neil McLeod, 'The blood-feud in medieval Ireland' in Pamela O'Neill (ed.), *Between intrusions: Britain and Ireland between the Romans and the Normans* (Sydney: University of Sydney, 2004), pp 114–33, esp. 124–5. **35** Adomnán, in his *Life of Columba,* however, deliberately diminished the saint's partisanship for his Uí Néill kin; see Michael Meckler, 'Kinship in Adomnán's *Vita s. Columbae*' in Dorothea Walz (ed.), *Scripturus vitam: lateinische Biographie von der Antike bis in die Gegenwart* (Heidelberg: Mattes, 2002), pp 723–30.

Emerging from the Bushes: the Welsh Law of Women in the Legal Triads

SARA ELIN ROBERTS

The Welsh law of women, published in 1980, was a groundbreaking work in many ways.[1] It was the first full study of an individual tractate of Welsh law, and the first in a series of such studies.[2] Each book brought together the latest research in the field of Welsh law, and presented up-to-date texts with translations for different versions of the tractates. *The Welsh law of women* is the standard work on the subject, and the first point of reference for anyone wishing to look at women in medieval Wales.

Far-reaching as the book is, the volume is a study of the law of women tractate in the Welsh laws, rather than a study of women in the whole corpus of Welsh law. This is an obvious and sensible way of approaching the subject: the lawyers organized their material into separate sections, and the tractate was intended to be the discussion on women in the laws. However, the laws were not a solid, static thing (much as the lawyers may have wished it to be so), but developed over time. New material was added, older parts became obsolete, and the rules would have been changed according to custom or usefulness.[3] There does not seem to be much development in the law of women tractate, although the law did keep developing. However, material could be added to the Welsh legal tractates in different ways. Sometimes additional laws or information would be added at the end of a tractate: an example of this is the additional material found at the end of the *galanas* section of the three columns tractate.[4] Alternatively, a tail of material would

1 D. Jenkins and M.E. Owen (eds), *The Welsh law of women* (Cardiff: University of Wales Press, 1980) [*WLW*]. 2 The other studies are T.M. Charles-Edwards, M.E. Owen, and D.B. Walters (eds), *Lawyers and laymen* (Cardiff: University of Wales Press, 1980); T.M. Charles-Edwards, M.E. Owen, and P. Russell (eds), *The Welsh king and his court* (Cardiff: University of Wales Press, 2000) [*WKC*]. A fourth study on the three columns of law will appear in 2008. 3 For example, the laws of court in Welsh law became obsolete fairly early on, and by the fifteenth-century they were not copied into the lawbooks. *WKC*, pp 15–16. 4 S.J. Williams and J.E. Powell (eds), *Llyfr Blegywryd* (Cardiff: University of Wales Press, 1942), p. 31 [Bleg]; the practice is more common in Iorwerth; see A.Rh. Wiliam (ed.), *Llyfr Iorwerth* (Cardiff: University of Wales Press, 1960) [Ior], for the 'miscellaneous'

CSANA Yearbook 7: Four Courts Press, Dublin; ISSN 1649–0096; ISBN 978–1–84682–099–1

be added, taken from other redactions of the laws or material in certain forms; this method has been much discussed in the context of fifteenth-century Welsh legal compilations.[5] This additional material would often be in the form of triads, or in the case of the Iorwerth redaction, as *damweiniau*.[6] Aneurin Owen's second volume of *Ancient laws and institutes of Wales*, which he subtitled the 'anomalous laws', is mainly additional material, not found in the main tractates of Welsh law.[7] Studies of certain genres of the additional material do exist.[8] Therefore, a more complete study of the Welsh law of women tractate needs to take into account the additional material on women found within other tractates of the law – for example, the text discussing the queen's rights and responsibilities in the law of court, and material within the *damweiniau*, and in the legal triads, which is the focus of this paper.

This paper will concentrate on a selection of triads relating to the Welsh law of women from the legal manuscripts. The legal triad collections are exactly that – collections of triads useful to the medieval Welsh lawyers, the connection between every triad in the collection being Welsh law. Welsh law, however, is a huge subject, and so classifying the triads in the collections according to subject is no easy matter (especially as some triads combine three separate areas of law), although 'runs' of triads on the same topic often occur.

There are four redactions, or groups, of Welsh law manuscripts, each demonstrating differences and regional variation, although many of the same tractates occur in each of the redactions. The Latin manuscripts are the loosest grouping of the four redactions, although the five Latin versions are linked to each other, and there are similarities between the Latin laws and the Welsh redactions. Of the three Welsh groups, Cyfnerth probably retains the earliest version of the Welsh laws, although most of the manuscripts are fourteenth-century in date; the material is probably older than the manuscripts.[9] The Blegywryd redaction, a translation of a version of Latin D, like Cyfnerth, derives from south Wales and is the latest of the three groups, as well as the largest.[10] Iorwerth could be classed as the north Wales redaction,

sections throughout the list of contents. pp xliii–xliv. **5** For example, see A.Rh. Wiliam, 'Y deddfgronau Cymraeg', *National Library of Wales Journal* 8 (1953), 97–103, for a discussion on these later manuscripts with tails of additional material. **6** For the *damweiniau*, see D. Jenkins (ed.), *Damweiniau Colan* (Aberystwyth: Cymdeithas Lyfrau Ceredigion, 1973). **7** A. Owen (ed.), *Ancient Laws and Institutes of Wales*, 2 vols (London: Record Commission, 1841). **8** T.M. Charles-Edwards, 'Cynghawsedd: counting and pleading in medieval Welsh law', *Bulletin of the Board of Celtic Studies* 33 (1984), 188–98; R.C. Stacey, 'Learning to plead in medieval Welsh law', *Studia Celtica* 38 (2004), 107–23; *Damweiniau Colan*; S.E. Roberts, 'Plaints in mediaeval Welsh law', *Journal of Celtic Studies* 4 (2004), 219–61; and S.E. Roberts, *The legal triads of medieval Wales* (Cardiff: University of Wales Press, 2007) [*LT*]. **9** For an edited text and discussion of the Cyfnerth manuscripts, see A.W. Wade-Evans, *Welsh Medieval law* (Oxford: Clarendon Press, 1909; repr. Aalen: Scientia, 1979) [Cyfn]. **10** The relationship between Latin D and Bleg are discussed by H. D. Emanuel, 'Llyfr Blegywryd a

containing the earliest manuscripts, although the law seems to reflect the legal situation in Gwynedd during the time of Llywelyn the Great.[11] For this study, the spotlight will not be on Iorwerth, as the Iorwerth manuscripts do not contain a large collection of triads, but only triads within the tractates.[12] The Bleg and Cyfn manuscripts, however, do contain large triad collections, with some of the Cyfn manuscripts showing a core collection, contained within the larger Bleg collection.[13] All but two of the triads (Q118 and Q119) from the triad collection studied here all occur in both Cyfn and Bleg, and they occur in the core collection in Cyfn, thus taken into Bleg. Their content is usually the same, with the occasional change in wording, with no notable additions or omissions. The Bleg text from Q will be used here.[14]

The development of the triad collections is a complex subject, and has been discussed more fully elsewhere,[15] but a quick summary may be useful here. It does not seem that one person set out to compose triads in bulk, creating the Bleg collection of over a hundred triads; indeed, the triad collection is unlikely to have been composed as a collection, with over a hundred triads composed in one sitting. This is also true of most of the tractates – several layers of development can be seen within most tractates of Welsh law, and additions and emendations were made over the course of time. Triad collections probably originated as mnemonic aids, of practical use to the lawyers as a ready-reference to the main points of Welsh law. A large collection is found in all Cyfnerth and Blegywryd redaction manuscripts.[16] The triad collections can be classed as a separate tractate in the laws in their own right. The Iorwerth manuscripts have a very small collection of a dozen or so triads, but it is more common to see a large collection of *damweiniau* in manuscripts of that redaction.[17] With the triad collections, it is more likely that a small group was gathered early on – this can be seen in the Iorwerth texts[18] – and then added to with time, drawing together triads from oral tradition, and later from other parts of the lawbooks, to create what became eventually a large collection.[19] By the time of the Cyfnerth manuscripts, there was a 'core' collection of triads on various subjects, which found their way in bulk, often keeping the same order, into the Bleg collection which is much larger.[20]

Llawysgrif Rawlinson 821', *Bulletin of the Board of Celtic Studies*, 29 (1962–4), 23–8, and he published the text in H.D. Emanuel (ed.), *The Latin texts of the Welsh laws* (Cardiff: University of Wales Press, 1967) [*LTWL*]. **11** *LT*, pp 2–3. **12** The short Ior collection of eleven triads focuses on status and the laws of court, and there are no triads on the law of women within this group. **13** *LT*, p. 22. **14** The rationale for using manuscript Q, NLW Wynnstay 36, is set out in *LT*, p. ix. **15** *LT*, pp 15–30. **16** *LT*, pp 1–3. **17** I intend to discuss this material more fully elsewhere in an article on the Iorwerth triads. **18** Ior, §42. **19** *LT*, p. 27. **20** *LT*, pp 22 and 24.

Important evidence on the growth of the triad collections is found in Latin D. The surviving Latin D manuscript contains a text similar to that found in the Bleg manuscripts – the Bleg manuscripts were a translation of a Latin D text – but it is not the exact text translated into Welsh to become Blegywryd, and it is more likely to be a branch from the same stem.[21] In Latin D, there are two large triad collections: the Cyfn core collection (slightly adapted), and another collection of triads mainly focusing on procedure.[22] These two triad collections were combined and became the one large triad collection in the Bleg manuscripts.[23] So, in the case of legal procedure, there was a collection of triads all focusing on the same subject. This is not true in the case of the law of women, and the triads on the law of women are found scattered throughout the Cyfn core collection in Latin D. Crucially, we can see the process of creating the triad collection happening, by the combination of two blocks of triads. It happened sometime between the compilation of the surviving Latin D manuscript and the first Bleg manuscript: in the surviving Latin D manuscript, the triads are found at the end of the tractate on the duties and responsibilities of a justice, as a collection of procedural triads, but appended to a relevant section of text.[24]

Triads were often inserted at relevant points into the main tractates of Welsh law, and this is true of both the Bleg and the Cyfn law of women tractate.[25] There are three triads found in the Bleg women tractate, but the Cyfn manuscripts show more variation: X, Mk, W and Z have the same two triads: one is the same as Q232 and is in the same position in the tractate, and the other is the same as Q119, found in the triad collection in Bleg. Z, Mk and W have the same third triad in the women tractate, and it is the same as Q234; these three Cyfn manuscripts are often closer to Bleg. Manuscript V is no longer complete; parts of the law of women tractate are missing, and there are no triads in the surviving portion. Manuscript U has a tractate unlike any of the other Cyfn manuscripts and it contains no triads.[26] As the Bleg manuscripts are more stable in terms of content and form where triads are concerned, this study will focus on the Bleg triads, with reference to Cyfnerth where applicable.

In some tractates of Welsh law, short collections of triads are found together, e.g. the land law tractate. In the law of women in Bleg, two of the

21 *LT*, pp 26–9. **22** *LT*, pp 26–7. **23** *LT*, p. 27. **24** *LTWL*, p. 349; 'de diversis iudicibus' and the triads are found on pp 354–7. **25** Several of the Iorwerth triads in the *Ior* women tractate are unique to Ior, and none occur in the women tractate in Bleg and Cyfn, or in the main triad collections in those redactions, but most Iorwerth triads turn up in fifteenth-century extended *Bleg* manuscripts. One of the seven Iorwerth triads in the women tractate is incorporated into the extended triad collection in manuscript Q, from the fifteenth century, in an extended form, although the concept is found in another triad in the main Bleg collection. There seems to be very little contact between the Iorwerth triads and the main Bleg collection, as they only occur in later Bleg manuscripts, if at all. **26** *WLW*, pp 132–4.

triads are consecutive, both discussing payments due to women. They follow other references to payments due to women, and so summarize points made in the surrounding text.[27] It is also interesting that there are only three triads in the Bleg tractate; triads are common in Welsh legal tractates. Three is a relatively low number: for example, in the short text on justice and justiceship, there are ten triads, and there is a small collection of triads grouped together after the tractate on land law.[28] It could equally be argued that the number of triads on land law and the justice is unusually high, but the actual nature of the triads in the Bleg women tractate makes the low number interesting.

Two of the three triads could be called 'procedural' triads: Q233 and Q234 give certain legal situations which can be divided into three – in other words, one legal situation is divided into three stages rather than having a triad combining three different ideas or circumstances. It could be said that these two triads are purely mnemonic, for easy recollection of the procedures.

> Q233. Teir g6eith y keiff g6reic y h6yneb6erth: yn gyntaf 6heugeint, yr eil 6eith punt, y tryded 6eith y dicha6n ada6 y g6r, a mynet a'e holl dylyet genthi, ac os diodef hi dros y tryded 6eith, ny cheiff hi y h6yneb6erth.
>
> Three times a woman receives her *wynebwerth*: the first time six score, the second time a pound, the third time she may leave her husband and go with all of her entitlement with her, and if she suffers beyond the third time, she does not receive her *wynebwerth*.

Q233, on paying *wynebwerth* compensation to a woman, has one situation – the woman is owed compensation – but three different results or procedures to follow, with the *wynebwerth* payment increasing each time her husband causes her an insult. The lawyer would need to remember the three increases, but otherwise there is only one situation in the triad – *wynebwerth* is due.

> Q234. Tri ll6 a dyry g6reic y 6r: pan enllipper gyntaf, ll6 seith 6raged, ac yr eil enllip, ll6 pedeir g6raged ar dec, a'r trydyd enllip, ll6 deg 6raged a deu vgeint, o byd neb ry6 hyspysr6yd ar yr enllip.
>
> Three oaths a wife is to give to her husband: when first accused, she is to give the oath of seven women, upon the second accusation, the oaths of fourteen women, upon the third, the oaths of fifty women, if there be any certainty behind the accusation.

27 Bleg, pp 78.24–80.6; for the three triads in the women tractate, see *LT*, Q232, Q233 and Q234.
28 Bleg, pp 98.28–105.17; 78.24–80.6.

Q234, on the three oaths a woman may give to her husband, is similarly 'functional' – the number of women needed to support the oath increases each time, and so the lawyer would need to memorize the number of women with two increases, but the situation again stays the same. This does not tell us anything about the situation or status of women in the Welsh laws. The triad is functional in that it would be extremely useful to a medieval lawyer needing to know off pat the number of women needed to support an oath. The triad does not contain surprising information – each time a woman needs to swear an oath, the number of supporting women increases.

The other triad in the women tractate in Bleg, however, is more interesting. It is the first triad in that tractate, and it also occurs in Cyfn in a similar place, which suggests that the triad was part of the women tractate from an early stage, at least from the time of Cyfn, the oldest redaction, and it may be part of the original material on women in the Welsh laws.[29]

> Q232. O tri acha6s ny chyll g6reic y heg6edi kyt ada6o y g6r: o glafri, ac o eisseu kyt, a dryc anadyl.
>
> For three reasons a woman does not lose her *agweddi*, although she leaves her husband: for leprosy, and for want of intercourse, and for bad breath.

The triad is on *agweddi*, a share of the matrimonial property, decided when a couple first got married, which went to the wife if her husband left her before seven years of marriage; it was a sort of insurance payment for a woman who was left by her husband.[30] The triad gives the three situations where a woman is paid her *agweddi*, although she herself leaves her husband. Normally, if a woman left her husband of her own accord, she would not receive her *agweddi*, but the three cases given in the triad are just causes for leaving a husband. They are impotence, leprosy and bad breath. The first would have serious consequences, as the main reason for marriage was to produce offspring. Leprosy was viewed as dangerous and contagious (so the woman would probably be reluctant to attempt intercourse), and meant that the man would not survive and would be unlikely to father children. The last case may seem surprising, but may again have a link to impotence: apart from making sexual intercourse unpleasant, bad breath could be an indicator of more serious disease, such as a respiratory infection, kidney or liver disease and untreated diabetes, all incurable in the middle ages. However, Fergus Kelly notes that the Irish triads often have a punchline or humorous third item; this triad may be an example of medieval humour.[31]

29 *LT*, Q232, X9. **30** *WLW*, pp 187–8. **31** F. Kelly, 'Thinking in threes: the triad in early Irish literature', *Proceedings of the British Academy* 125 (2003), 1–18 at 10–12.

Turning to the triad collection in Bleg, there are several triads on the subject of the law of women, and other triads discuss the related subjects of children and inheritance. These latter triads are particularly interesting as there is no separate tractate on children and inheritance in the Bleg texts; material on children is found as a short tractate in the Iorwerth manuscripts, so the triads are supplying the material on children in the Bleg texts.[32] There are many triads on the subject of women in the Bleg triad collection, and this may be telling, given that there are only three triads within the women tractate; there seems to be an interest in the law of women in the triads.

Eight triads in the Bleg stand out as discussing only the law of women. Although the triads in the main Bleg collection appear to be a jumble, there are attempts at ordering the triads by subject, a system also found in the Cyfn triad collections and probably reflecting the triads' original purpose as mnemonics.[33] Often, there are contrasting pairs, or sets of triads which belong together; occasionally, there are groups of consecutive triads on the same subject.[34] The triads I will be discussing are numbered according to the order in which they appear in manuscript Q (the order is the same in all of the Bleg manuscripts) and the numbering of the triads shows that several of them, on the law of women, are consecutive, so this supports the idea of subject-grouping within the triad collection.

The first triad which deserves attention does not at first glance appear to be discussing women, but rather sons and inheritance – Q71 is the first in a short run of triads on the law of women, on the three women whose sons are entitled to the inheritance of their mother; but there is an attempt to put the situation from the women's point of view, as the triad lists the three women, rather than the three sons.[35] The opening words are different in Cyfn, and it may have been adapted by the time of Bleg to reflect the true content of the triad – the law of women, rather than sons and inheritance.[36]

> Q71. Teir g6raged a dyly eu meibon tref eu mam: g6reic a rother tros y that yng g6ystyl, a chaffel mab ohonei yn y g6ystyloryaeth; a g6reic a rother o rod kenedyl y alltut; a g6reic a lather g6r o'e chenedyl, a dial o'e mab h6nn6, ny dylyir y oedi am tref y vam, nac aros nauetdyd yn y erbyn.
>
> Three women whose sons are entitled to the inheritance of their mother: a woman who is given as a hostage on behalf of her father, and she has a son during that hostageship; and a woman who is given by gift of kin to an alien; and a woman from whose kindred a man is killed, and her son avenges him, there should be no delaying him concerning the inheritance of his mother, nor waiting until the ninth day to receive it.

32 Ior, §§97–103. **33** *LT*, p. 10. **34** *LT*, pp 10–11. **35** *LT*, Q71. **36** *LT*, X30.

Women were not entitled to hold land in Welsh law, and they ordinarily would not have land to pass on, so the situation in this triad is highly unusual.[37] However, there are good reasons why the sons would receive land through the mother's side. It becomes clear that the three men would not be entitled to land through their fathers according to Welsh law, since two appear to be the sons of aliens (non-Welshmen) – and aliens, like women, had no right to land.[38] Anyone who did not have Welsh status was in a bad situation in Welsh law, but the two men in this triad have alien fathers as their mothers were not treated carefully enough by their own kindred: in the case of a woman given by gift of kin in marriage to an alien, her own kindred put her in a situation where her sons would not be able to inherit land, and therefore this triad makes provision for a son whose grandparents and relatives might have set up for problems by choosing a husband unwisely for a kinswoman.

It is not clear in the second case, that of a woman given as a hostage having a son whilst being kept hostage, whether the father of her son was an alien, but it seems to be implied, as, according to Welsh law, the status of the union is of no consequence as long as the father acknowledges his own sons.[39] Therefore, for a son to have no inheritance, it seems that his father was also an alien. There is an implication that the woman was raped while a hostage, or else she has taken matters into her own hands and has become pregnant with one of her captors. Either way, her kindred were foolish to give a woman of marriageable age as a hostage, possibly ruining her chances of securing a good union. If it was rape, then they had rendered her and themselves vulnerable in a situation where sexual vulnerability is coincident with political vulnerability.

The third case in the triad, the son who avenges a killing from his mother's kindred, would lose his patrimony as a punishment for taking revenge, killing another. This may be in the context of the other two limbs in the triad, and that the boy's father was an alien, but in that case he would have a claim as he would be defending the kindred of his mother. Alternatively, the killer may have come from his father's kindred, and the son has then put his paternal inheritance at risk by defending his mother's kindred against his father's. Either way, according to this triad, he has lost his inheritance through his own kindred, his father's side, but the law reverts to his mother's kindred. It is unclear why; perhaps showing loyalty to his mother's kindred was considered to be a positive thing, even though his mother was no longer part of that kin-group. In any other situation of revenge, the person committing the act of revenge would lose his patrimony;

37 Ior, §86/1. **38** D. Jenkins, *Hywel Dda: the law* (Llandysul: Gwasg Gomer, 1986), pp 114–22. **39** Jenkins, *Hywel Dda: the law*, pp 135–7.

the only situation where this would not be the case would be where compensation had not been received – according to Welsh law someone was either entitled to compensation (preferable) or could take revenge (worst-case scenario).[40] Each of these cases is interesting, as they tell us a fair amount about the status of women. It appears that they had no say in their marriages, and were at the mercy of their families – if the family gave a woman away to an alien, or seemingly ruined her chances at a decent match, there was not a great deal she could do about it. However, according to this triad, the sons' inheritance would be safeguarded.

The next triad in the group of four on women in the Bleg triad collection is on the three *sarhaeds* of a woman, or the three cases where a woman would receive the *sarhaed* payment, compensation for an insult or a deliberate act.[41]

> Q24. Teir sarhaet g6reic ynt, vn a drycheif, ac vn a ost6g, ac vn ysyd sarhaet g6byl: kyntaf y6 bot genthi o'e hanuod, a honno gan vn drychafel y telir idi. Yr eil y6 rodi cussan idi o'e hanuod, a honno a ost6g, y trayan a vyd eisseu idi. Trydyd y6 y phaluu o'e hanuod, a honno yssyd sarhaet g6byl idi; ac os g6rya6c vyd, her6yd breint y g6r y telir idi.
>
> These are the three *sarhaeds* of a woman, one which is augmented, one which is decreased, and one which is complete *sarhaed*: the first is to have intercourse with her against her will, and that is paid to her with one augmentation. The second is to give her a kiss against her will, and that is decreased, a third is lacking from it. The third is to grope her against her will, and that is complete *sarhaed* to her; and if she is married, it is paid to her according to the status of her husband.

In most of the Bleg manuscripts, this triad would be found in the triad collection, but manuscript Q has re-edited the text and moved the triad, along with others, into the three columns of law tractate, dealing with *galanas* (the homicide payment) and the accompanying *sarhaed* payment.[42] Ordinarily, it would fit between Q71 and Q72 in the Bleg collection. According to the law of women, the husband would receive the *sarhaed* compensation on behalf of his wife – she was treated as part of her husband's property.[43] However, this triad shows a different situation – the woman herself receives the payment in these instances. There is a crucial element – the woman is unwilling according to the triad, and kissing, groping or raping her is an assault on her body. In the main tractate in Bleg, the situation is that

40 *LT*, p. 249. **41** *LT*, Q24; see also the note for X31. **42** *LT*, p. 32. **43** M.E. Owen, 'Shame and reparation: woman's place in the kin' in *WLW*, pp 40–68 at 53.

the woman was a participant in these three cases, and so it would be an insult to her husband, but as she is unwilling in the triad, she has some rights over her own body. The *sarhaed* is increased or decreased according to the seriousness: having sexual intercourse with her against her will is the basic *sarhaed* payment plus an increase; groping her against her will (the word *palfu* implies some violence and roughness, with an element of internal groping, rather than simply touching inappropriately)[44] is full *sarhaed*, and kissing her against her will would be worth less than her full *sarhaed*. The triad is giving us a situation which is not prominent in the women tractate in Bleg, and in the triad the woman has some bodily integrity if attacked.

The next triad, Q72, takes this concept further.

> Q72. Tri che6ylid kenedyl ynt ac o acha6s g6reic y maent: llathrudra6 o'e hanuod; eil y6 d6yn o'r g6r 6reic arall ar y pen y'r ty; trydyd y6 y hyspeila6.
>
> These are the three shames of a kindred and they are because of a woman: abducting her against her will; the second is if her husband brings another woman to the house to encounter her; the third is to despoil her.

The three shames of a kindred makes the offences or attacks against a woman serious to the whole kin group, and although it is still paternalistic, it shows a sense of responsibility towards women not found in the women tractate in the redactions – the whole kindred should feel responsible, and if a woman was injured or treated badly, they would all be party to the shame.[45] However, the basis for this responsibility may be financial – 'damage' to a woman could cost a kindred – and so selfish, rather than sensitivity to her feelings.[46] Two of the three incidents listed in the triad are direct attacks: abducting her (presumably for some sexual gratification later), and despoiling her; *ysbeilio* is a strange word to use in this context and it is used in all versions of the triad. In the earlier Welsh examples of *ysbeilio* in *GPC*, it can mean to strip someone of their clothes, and this is supported by the *Oxford English dictionary*, 'despoil'.[47] In the triad it may simply mean stripping a woman of her clothing, or it may have a wider meaning of taking something violently from the woman – a *sarhaed* to the queen, according to the laws of court.[48] The use of *ysbeilio* for rape is not found, although it may

44 *Geiriadur Prifysgol Cymru* (Cardiff: University of Wales Press, 1967–2002), p. 2673, *s.v. palfalaf: palfalu, palfala, palfalad*. [*GPC*] **45** *LT*, Q72, and see the note on X33. **46** K.M. Phillips, 'Written on the body: reading rape from the twelfth to fifteenth centuries' in N.J. Menuge (ed.), *Medieval women and the law* (Woodbridge: Boydell Press, 2000), pp 125–44 at 142–4. **47** *GPC*, pp 3822–3, *s.v. ysbeiliaf*². **48** *LT*, Q3.

mean something similar here, and a sense of violence is strongly implied in the word.[49]

The third item in the triad is when her husband takes a new wife, while still married to the original woman, and the two women meet. This is, unsurprisingly, quite shameful to the woman, but again implies that the whole kindred should be protective and ensure that the man does not do things which would harm her; it seems that marriage is not such a private matter when it comes to personal shame or injury in Welsh law. In another triad, the woman would be allowed to kill the new woman without consequences.[50]

There is an element of humour in the next triad, although the legal concept found within it is sophisticated.[51]

> Q73. Tri chadarn enllip g6reic ynt: vn y6 g6elet y g6r a'r 6reic yn dyuot o'r vn ll6yn vn o pop parth y'r ll6yn, eil y6 eu kaffel ell deu dan vn vantell, trydyd y6 g6elet y g6r r6g deu uord6yt y 6reic.
>
> These are the three strong scandals of a woman: one is seeing the man and the woman emerging from the same bush one on either side of the bush, the second is finding them both under one blanket, the third is seeing the man between the two thighs of the woman.

Enllib in the modern sense means 'slander', and the word is not attested in the laws outside of this triad. The triad gives the three cases where the woman can be accused of adultery, and in each of the three, it is pretty clear what has been happening, even though actual adultery was not witnessed. This triad is presenting situations where the court could act on a presumption that adultery had taken place, short of direct evidence (such as confession or eye-witness testimony). This triad is setting out a concept not found elsewhere in Welsh law, showing that Welsh law was not only a system reaching conclusions based on direct evidence, but a system which could also reach a conclusion, in appropriate circumstances, from evidence that strictly speaking falls short of full proof of adultery but which it is unlikely to be unjust to rely upon.

On the whole, the Welsh law of evidence is pretty mysterious, the problem being due in no small part to the lack of surviving evidence on the Welsh laws in actual practice. In short, the lawbooks tell us about oaths, which were the main way of proving anything in Welsh law, as in other legal systems from the same period.[52] Dafydd Jenkins, in his discussion on this

49 *LT*, p. 257. **50** *LT*, Q106, and see the discussion, above. **51** *LT*, Q73. **52** D. Jenkins, *Cyfraith Hywel* (Llandysul: Gwasg Gomer, 1976), p. 101.

aspect of Welsh law, contrasts the situation today, where an oath in court would be for giving evidence, rather than being used to support someone else's oath. The number of people giving oaths, and the type of oath given, could vary according to the situation or the need.[53] However, this depends on the case getting to the court in the first place – a different type of evidence perhaps to that needed to accuse a person and bring forward a legal case. It seems that any legal case in medieval Wales would open with a plaint to the lord or king, a legal statement setting out the situation and making clear that someone has committed a wrongdoing, and how the victim has suffered and what is expected as a result.[54] In that case, it is assumed that there are witnesses who can give evidence to prove that the situation, as set out in the plaint, is true. Welsh law details different witnesses: the nine tongued-ones, a list of nine people whose evidence, in certain situations, would be believed over any other evidence.[55] Then there are the two basic types of witnesses, the *ceidwaid* 'maintainers', who would maintain someone's claim to something, and the *gwybyddiaid* 'knowers', actual eyewitnesses.[56] These witnesses are most often seen in discussions on land law and property law in medieval Wales. The witnesses and those making an oath in a court would be swearing that what they saw – or what another person had said – was actually true.[57] What the lawbooks do not tell us, however, is how people would get to that stage – naturally someone had to see something, and be willing to swear as to the truth of it.

This triad gives us one further stage into the process by telling us the nature of what had to be seen. In cases of adultery, the witness would need to see certain things for the evidence to be strong enough to take a case to court (or settle the matter in another way) – and the three strong scandals in the triad seem to be the three clear cases where a woman can be accused of adultery, because she has been seen in a situation which would make it hard for her to deny that she was having intercourse with a man other than her husband. So, in this triad, we have some signs as to how the law would be used and the evidence needed to bring a case against a woman. Although the triad may seem simplistic, there is sophisticated legal thinking behind it, and the short triad is an important part of the material on the actual practice of law in medieval Wales.

Following this triad, there are more on the subject of children and inheritance, and claiming or rejecting children of doubtful parentage; the subject of children or sons, in particular, is closely related to the law of women, and it maintains the subject grouping found within the triad

53 Ibid., p. 101. **54** Roberts, 'Plaints in mediaeval Welsh law', 220–1. **55** Jenkins, *Cyfraith Hywel*, p. 102. **56** Ibid., 103–4. **57** Thomas Glyn Watkin, *The legal history of Wales* (Cardiff: University of Wales Press, 2007), p. 74.

collection. However, as this study is focusing primarily on women, we can jump to Q26, another of the 'moved' triads in manuscript Q, which would ordinarily be found following Q75 and before a triad on denying doubtful children from a kindred.[58]

> Q26. Tri g6erth kyfreith beichogi g6reic: vn y6 g6aet kyn del6at, 6yth a deu vgeint a tal or collir tr6y greulonder. Eil y6 kyn dyuot eneit ynda6, or collir tr6y greulonder trayan galanas a telir ymdana6. Trydyd y6 g6edy yd el eneit ynda6, talu c6byl o'e alanas a dylyir or collir tr6y greulonder.
>
> Three legal values of a woman's foetus: one is blood before formation, if it is lost through cruelty it is worth forty-eight [pence]. The second is before life enters it, if it is lost through cruelty a third of the *galanas* is paid for it. The third is after life enters it, its full *galanas* ought to be paid if it is lost through cruelty.

The only material in the Bleg and Cyfn manuscripts on the foetus, the triad differs to the material on the same subject found in *Ior*, but according to Morfydd Owen, it is closer to European tradition and canon law.[59] Again, the triad shows legal refinement: rather than have one payment for losing a pregnancy, the compensation is increased according to the advancement of the pregnancy. It is assumed that the payment would go to the woman, or at least to the parents of the unborn baby, and it may therefore reflect the parents' attachment to the growing child.

Possibly one of the most interesting triads on the subject of women is not found as part of the consecutive group within the collection, and the main focus of the triad – at least in the heading – is not on women at all, but on thrusts for which there is no compensation.[60]

> Q106. Tri h6rd ny di6ygir: vn y6 h6rd g6r ac aryf yn y elyn am y gar g6edy ys gofynho yn tri dadleu, a heb gaffel ia6n; kyt as llado, nys di6c. Eil y6 h6rd g6reic 6rya6c yn y chy6yres a'e d6y la6 yn y kyfarffont; kyt bo mar6, ny di6ygir. Trydyd y6 o rodir t6ylluor6yn y 6r, a g6edy y phroui y chaffel yn t6ylluor6yn, a mach ar y mor6ynda6t; kyt as g6anho a'e la6 neu a'e troet dros y g6ely ac nas llado, nys di6c. Yr h6rd heuyt a 6anho a bonllost yndi ny di6ygir idi; llather y chrys, hagen, yn gyfu6ch a thal y phedrein, a'r tu racdi yn gyfu6ch a g6arr y chont, a'e gell6g a'r h6rd h6nn6 yndi heb y diu6yn idi. A hynny y6 kyfreith t6ylluor6yn.

58 *LT*, Q26, and the note on X39. **59** M.E. Owen, 'Medics and medicine' in *WKC*, pp 116–41 at 131–2. **60** *LT*, Q106 and the note on X55.

> Three thrusts for which reparation is not made: one is the thrust of a man with a weapon into his enemy [in revenge] for his relative after he has asked [for redress] in three sessions, without receiving redress; although he may kill him, he does not pay compensation. The second is a thrust of a married woman at her [husband's] concubine with her two hands when they meet; although she may die, compensation is not paid. The third is if a false virgin is given to a man, and after testing her she is found to be a false virgin, with surety on her virginity; although he shoves her with his hand or his foot over the bed and does not kill her, he does not pay compensation. Also there is no redress to her for the thrust he made into her with his penis; however, let her shift be cut as high as the top of her buttocks, and in front as high as the top of her cunt, and she is released with that thrust in her without compensating her for it. And that is the law of a false virgin.

The first thrust is when a man strikes another, with a weapon, and kills him; in this case there is unpaid *galanas*, and the thrust is taking revenge, so this is reinforcing the idea that if compensation is not received, taking revenge is allowed, but only as the last resort. The second element of the triad does seem to refer to the law of women – it is a case where a married woman kills her husband's concubine with her hands, and this reflects an idea found in a previously discussed triad where the kindred should take care of the women and ensure that they are not ill-treated by their husbands, as it would bring shame on the whole kindred. The concubine and her family clearly have no rights in this situation.

The third element is by far the longest part of this triad and its length suggests that this was the main point which the redactor wanted to make; it may even be the case that the previous two situations were added to this one in order to make a triad. It also seems to be a separate tractate of law and is labelled as such – '*A hynny yw cyfraith twyllforwyn*'. Provision for virgins who turn out to have had intercourse with other men is found in the laws, and as the girl's family were required to supply a maiden as part of the marriage contract, it seems to have been a preoccupation.[61] In the law of women, if a girl is given to a man and on their wedding night he discovers that she is not a virgin, then she is entitled to swear to the validity of her virginity as one of five oath-swearers, including her close family.[62]

However, the law found in this triad is a different matter, and it is not found in the law of women in Bleg or Cyfn, and although similar material

61 A full discussion on this section of the triad can be found in N.W. Patterson, 'Honour and shame in medieval Welsh society: a study of the role of burlesque in the Welsh laws', *Studia Celtica* 16–17 (1981–2), 71–103 at 73–9. **62** Bleg, p. 64.11–17.

is found in Ior, there are very subtle differences. In the women tractate in Bleg, and Cyfn, the man may accuse his new bride of not being a virgin, and she may swear that she is, in fact, a virgin; in Ior, she is punished if she does not wish to clear her name (either way, not an auspicious start to any marriage!).[63] The difference in this triad is that the oath has *already* been sworn on her virginity, and surety has even been given: the husband is expecting a guaranteed virgin, but discovers that his wife is not a virgin, so there has been some deception and even lies, as someone is passing off this woman as a virgin when she is not. The woman herself is punished, as she is part of the deception, and the triad is cleverly constructed with the three thrusts: first, a weapon; then bare hands; and finally the man's penis (although he is also allowed to beat her or kick her, and there is no punishment for that either). The girl's punishment is cruel and humiliating, and does not show Welsh law in a good light, as far as the treatment of women is concerned. However, the triad is important as it offers material not found elsewhere in the law manuscripts, and not included in the women tractate in Bleg, Cyfn or Ior, and the triad gives the situation, a description of how to state the case in some versions, and her punishment, in full. If the first two elements were in fact added in an attempt to create a triad – and there is evidence of this happening elsewhere – we have another example of the triad form being used as a way of presenting original material, either arising from regional variation, or demonstrating innovation and historical development.[64]

The final two triads for consideration are consecutive in the Bleg triad collection, although they do not form a natural pair, and although both are on the law of women, they are separate triads.[65]

> Q118. Tri chy6ilyd mor6yn yssyd: vn y6 dy6edut o'e that 6rthi 'mi a'th rodeis y 6r'; eil y6 pan el gyntaf y g6ely y g6r; trydyd y6 pan el gyntaf o'r g6ely ym plith dynyon. Dros y kyntaf y rodir y hamobyr y'r argl6yd; dros yr eil y rodir y chy6yll idi hitheu; dros y trydyd y dyry tat y heg6edi y'r g6r.
>
> There are three shames of a maiden: one is when her father tells her 'I have given you to a man'; the second is when she goes for the first time to her husband's bed; the third is when she goes for the first time from the bed amongst men. For the first her *amobr* is given to the lord; for the second her *cowyll* is given to her; for the third the father gives her *agweddi* to the husband.

63 *WLW*, Ior text 47/2–5. **64** See also H. Pryce, *Native law and the church in medieval Wales* (Oxford: Oxford University Press, 1993), pp 101–5, where he argues convincingly that one triad combines a legal idea from the time of Henry II, a rule referring to canon law and reflecting the Norman reformers' attempt to enforce clerical celibacy (again later in date), and a third element which rests uneasily; the triad form could be used to introduce new legal ideas into Welsh law. **65** Some triads

Q118 is, according to Morfydd Owen, an attempt to explain the exchanges of property which occurred during a marriage contract as reparation for the shame, or rather embarrassment, the woman would feel: a young girl might be embarrassed on being told that she had a husband lined up for her, then on going to his bed for the first time, and then getting up afterwards, when everyone would know what the pair had been up to.[66] This concept, of compensation for the embarrassment, reflects an attempt to re-work legal concepts – the redactor was trying to fit the exchanges of property which occur into another framework and rationalizing them in terms of compensation. The three events are not necessarily shameful for a woman, and were probably considered to be a rite of passage – although in the period, the church was emphasising links between sexuality and shame-fulness, and a woman who was no longer a virgin (even if legitimately married) was not considered to be whole, but was now sexually polluted. The triad does, however, demonstrate some thought to the feelings of the woman; the young woman is being given in marriage and she does not have any say in it, and this triad shows a sensitivity not found in the women tractate in the redactions.

> Q119. Tri pheth ny ellir y d6yn rac g6reic kyt g6ahaner a hi am y cham: y cho6yll, a'e hargyfreu, a'e h6yneb6erth, os rygafas kyn hynny o gymryt o'e g6r 6reic arall yn y herbyn.
>
> Three things that cannot be taken from a woman though separation from her is caused by her misdeed: her *cowyll*, and her *argyfrau*, and her *wynebwerth*, if she had received them before then, because her husband took another woman in opposition to her.

Q119 is similar in that it lists three things (again given as part of the marriage contract) which a woman would keep no matter what, including in a situation where the husband leaves her because she has done something wrong. This looks highly unusual and is different to the material found in the women tractate in all of the redactions – normally, if a woman does something wrong, her husband may leave her and she does not get anything. The final section of the triad attempts to justify this, by saying that she had already received these three payments because her husband had taken on a new wife, so her crime occurred *after* she had been compensated, and he *then* left her.[67] This is very dubious, and the wording of the triad is unclear; it may be an attempt to outline once again the compensation or revenge situation –

form linked pairs or groups; *LT*, p. 10. **66** M.E. Owen, 'Shame and reparation: women's place in the kin' in *WLW*, pp 40–68 at 48–9. **67** *LT*, Q119.

perhaps the husband leaves her as revenge for some wrongdoing on her part, but this does not really work, as he had already done her wrong by taking the second wife. The addition to the triad may be a later effort to explain the strange situation, or even a clumsy attempt at correcting what appears to be an error. Wrong or unclear, it may show that there were expert readers at work on the triads, and as with the previous triad, this sentence may be a later addition, and we may have a triad made of different layers. The triad does not occur in Ior, but is found in the women tractate in Cyfn, but the triad in Cyfn ends at '*wynebwerth*' and does not include the last section attempting to explain the situation, which again may point to slightly later dating for that addition.

One aspect which has emerged from this study is that the Welsh law tractates were not static and fixed, but were added to, and 'new' or additional material was appended to them. Some triads were included in the Welsh legal tractates, and some tractates include a greater number of triads than others: for example, there are several triads on land law, and the two tractates on the justice and justiceship are largely comprised of triads with additional text in between.[68] (In contrast, there are no triads in the *mechnïaeth* tractate, but the Iorwerth tractate includes many *damweiniau*.)[69] In the case of contract law, there was a great deal of material to be added. The tractate of the law of women in each redaction, and between the redactions, is interesting in that it does not seem to show very much development: in each of the redactions, the material contained is much the same, with very few additional rules found between the different redactions.[70] To say that there was no development in the Welsh law of women would be wrong, however. Attitudes towards women and their rights did change, as it did elsewhere, probably with actual influence from outside Wales. However, the changes are not reflected in the women tractate in Bleg, which, as a text, is not rewritten to reflect the attitudes of the time. Rather, the changes to the law of women occur outside the tractate. One interesting point is the development of the role of the queen in the laws of court in Iorwerth.[71] The number of servants she has is increased, and her status is elevated; it has been suggested that this would have been done to reflect the situation when Llywelyn ap Iorwerth took Joan, daughter of King John of England, as his queen.[72] The law of women tractate stays the same in each redaction, but there were definite changes in the status and rights of the most high-ranking woman in Wales.

Where, then, does one turn to find further developments in the Welsh law of women? The answer may lie with the legal triads. The triads found in

68 Bleg, pp 17.19–18.21 and 98.28–106.17. **69** Ior, §§61–71 for the lists of sentences beginning *o derfydd* 'if it happens'. **70** See, for example, the discussion and table in *WLW*, pp 180–5. **71** R.C. Stacey, 'King, queen and *edling* in the laws of the court' in *WKC*, pp 29–62 at 55. **72** Ibid., pp 55–6.

the women tractate in Bleg are simplistic, and do not supply a great deal of information, but as demonstrated, the triads focusing on women found in the legal triad collections in Bleg do show a great deal of development. We see the idea of women as practically chattels in the women tractate in each redaction being re-thought, and the feelings of women being taken into consideration – for an assault on the body, a woman would receive compensation personally according to one triad, as she herself would have been injured, rather than have the compensation go directly to her husband. Admittedly, the main focus in the women tractate in all of the redactions is on how to compensate the husband when his wife messes about with other men. The triad may not be summarizing something brand new, and perhaps it was obvious to anyone that an attacked woman deserved compensation, but the fact is that the concept is actually spelt out, preserved in writing, and considered important enough to be treated in that way, within a triad. The rather clumsy reworking of the material on the exchanges during a marriage contract to represent payment for the embarrassment a girl would feel does actually show some concern for the feelings of a woman, however badly it was done, and it also shows that ideas were being reworked, and it could happen within triads. One of the triads gives a new section of law, or at least a material not contained within the women tractate or elsewhere in the law manuscripts – the law of *twyllforwyn* is labelled as a tractate, with labelling in this way often being used authoritatively for tractates. Rather than add this to the main tractate, it was included in a triad, and the triad may have been constructed especially to include this material; in that case, triads were seen as an appropriate way of including legal thinking into the lawtexts. Finally, the simple triad demonstrating the damning evidence of adultery is critical as far as the development of Welsh law is concerned – it shows that the Welsh lawyers were working at a higher level than basic rule-making, and that there was refinement to the legal process and adjustments to the way things were proved. One would expect nothing less of the medieval Welsh lawyers, and, as noted, the concept is not unique to medieval Welsh law – but the point is that the development was summarized again in a triad. Looking at the triads on the law of women is a useful method of looking at a cross-section of the Welsh law in general, and it can also tell us a great deal about the law of women – particularly as the tractate does not show a great deal of development, and also as there are very few triads in the women tractate.

The triads were part of what the medieval Welsh lawyer had to learn – it is generally stated that he would need to learn the value of wild and tame, the three columns of law and the practices of law.[73] However, dismissing the

73 S.E. Roberts, 'Addysg broffesiynol yng Nghymru yn yr oesoedd canol: y beirdd a'r cyfreithwyr', *Llên Cymru* 26 (2003), 1–17 at 11.

triad collections as only mnemonics would be oversimplification, as would reducing them to being merely literary forms. They are indeed both of these things, but it appears that the triads served a greater purpose in the mind of the Welsh lawyer, and the triad collections can be studies in their own right, as a melting pot for medieval Welsh legal thinking and further development of already sophisticated medieval Welsh law.

Derbforgaill's Literary Heritage: Can You Blame Her?[1]

LAHNEY PRESTON-MATTO

The story of the Norman invasion of Ireland is still a familiar one in the twenty-first century, and three key and well-storied Irish participants are usually judged as behaving badly: Derbforgaill is said to have betrayed her husband, Tigernán Ua Ruairc, king of Bréifne, to run away with Diarmaid Mac Murchada, king of Leinster. Mac Murchada and Ua Ruairc had been rivals for a long time before this, and continued to be rivals afterwards, a rivetingly nasty rivalry that contributed to Mac Murchada's eventual expulsion from Ireland, whereupon he went to Henry II of England for assistance. Henry in turn passed him on to his kinsmen in Wales, notably Richard fitz Gilbert, Lord of Strigoil, also known as Strongbow, whose marriage to Mac Murchada's daughter Aoife cemented a Leinster alliance with the Anglo-Normans and helped open the way for further Norman incursions.[2] In this article, I pursue Derbforgaill's story and how she comes to bear much of the blame for the Norman invasion of Ireland, as well as how her legal status as a wife affects that reputation.

By the nineteenth and twentieth centuries, Derbforgaill was seen by most Irish writers as responsible, in either small or large part, for the

1 Earlier versions of this article were presented as conference papers at the International Congress on Medieval Studies in Kalamazoo, Michigan in 2006 and 2007, as well as at the Harvard Celtic Colloquium in 2006. I received helpful feedback from all audiences, and would like to note in particular my gratitude to Charlene Eska, Marie Therese Flanagan, Patrick K. Ford, Catherine McKenna and Catherine Swift for their various suggestions and comments. I owe even larger thanks to Karen Overbey; working on such an interdisciplinary topic centered around one person has certainly widened my critical perspective, and this project progressed beyond what I originally envisioned due to our collaboration. 2 The events leading up to and following the Anglo-Normans' first *en masse* arrival in Ireland are well documented in the Annals of the four masters, the Annals of Tigernach, and the Annals of Clonmacnoise, as well as *The deeds of the Normans in Ireland*, to name a few of the more contemporary sources. See also Francis J. Byrne, *Irish kings and high-kings* (2nd ed.; Dublin: Four Courts Press, 2001), pp 273–4; Goddard Henry Orpen, *Ireland under the Normans 1169–1333* (Dublin: Four Courts Press, 2005), pp 1–64; and Marie Therese Flanagan, *Irish society, Anglo-Norman settlers, Angevin kingship* (Oxford: Clarendon Press, 1989), pp 56–112.

CSANA Yearbook 7: Four Courts Press, Dublin; ISSN 1649–0096; ISBN 978–1–84682–099–1

Norman invasion of Ireland. For example, Yeats emphasizes Derbforgaill's (and Mac Murchada's) search for forgiveness for their affair so that the erstwhile lovers may be reunited beyond the grave in his play *The dreaming of the bones*:

Dervorgilla: 'Yes, yes, I spoke
Of that most miserable, most accursed pair
Who sold their country into slavery; and yet
They were not wholly miserable and accursed
If somebody of their race at last would say,
"I have forgiven them."'
Young Man: 'O, never, never
Shall Diarmuid and Dervorgilla be forgiven.'[3]

At the end of the play, the Young Man, though sorely tempted, does not forgive Dervorgilla and Diarmuid, because he has recently fought in the Easter Rising in the GPO and perhaps blames his current difficulties, ultimately, on their actions seven hundred years before. James Joyce, too, underscores Derbforgaill's adultery via the Citizen in the Cyclops episode of *Ulysses*: 'A dishonoured wife, says the citizen, that's what's the cause of all our misfortunes.'[4] A few lines earlier, the Citizen has called Derbforgaill (without ever naming her) an 'adulteress' and Diarmaid her 'paramour' who brought the 'Saxon robbers' to Ireland.[5] Finally, Lady Gregory highlights Derbforgaill's continual penance for her adultery in her play *Dervorgilla*: 'Four years I have lived and fourscore, and for half my life I ran my own way, and through the other half of my life I have paid the penalty. For every day or night of pride or of pleasure, I have spent a day and a night of prayer and of pain. Will not that bring forgiveness? Is not that paying the penalty?'[6] The image of Derbforgaill as guilty party and penitent is extremely popular not only during the Celtic Revival, but also throughout the twentieth century.[7]

Of course, this image of Derbforgaill as responsible party had not been created from a vacuum. Thomas Moore includes a song called 'The valley lay smiling before me' in his wildly popular *Irish melodies* from the early nineteenth century. Told from Ua Ruairc's supposed point of view, Derbforgaill is named 'falsest of women' and 'degenerate daughter of Erin'. Ua Ruairc's

3 W.B. Yeats, *The dreaming of the bones*, in R. Alspach (ed.), *The variorum edition of the plays of W.B. Yeats* (New York: Macmillan, 1966), pp 762–76, lines 229–35. **4** James Joyce, *Ulysses* (New York: Vintage, 1990), p. 324. **5** Ibid. **6** Lady Gregory, *Dervorgilla*, in *Selected plays of Lady Gregory* (Washington: Colin Smythe, 1983), p. 156. **7** For further evidence of Derbforgaill's reception in the twentieth century, please see Karen Overbey's article in this volume, 'Female trouble: ambivalence and anxiety at the Nuns' Church,' where she cites two more recent and fairly amusing takes on Derbforgaill's reputation at the beginning of the section called 'The persistence of pathos'.

character also claims that 'thro' ages of bondage and slaughter,/ Our country shall bleed for thy shame.'[8] A short time after Moore wrote his version of a treacherous Derbforgaill, John Quincy Adams, inspired by David Hume's *The history of England*,[9] wrote a four canto poem called *Dermot MacMorrogh, or, The conquest of Ireland*, first published in 1832. Adams repeats throughout his introduction that 'history is the school of morals', so it is hardly surprising to find that his version of the story of Derbforgaill also stresses her faithlessness:

> [i]t is intended also as a moral tale, teaching the citizens of these States of both sexes, the virtues of conjugal fidelity, of genuine piety, and of devotion to their country, by pointing the finger of scorn at the example six hundred years since exhibited, of a country sold to a foreign invader by the joint agency of violated marriage vows, unprincipled ambition, and religious imposture.[10]

Adams' Derbforgaill is nothing if not vain: when Mac Murchada arrives to take her away, she feigns sleep, then demands half an hour to prepare, at which point she calls for her jewels and rouges her cheeks.[11] Adams does, however, mention the political implications of this abduction: knowing that her husband will face public speculation, derision, and possible opposition, Derbforgaill questions her maid, Agnes: '"what will people say," –/ Exclaim'd the lady with a briny flood;/ "If from the castle, while my lord's away/ I should depart; though to save shedding blood?"'[12] In order to help make the abduction seem more plausible, Adams has invented two treacherous servants – Agnes and Teague – as well as a visit to the entirely fictional Lady Ursula to account for Ua Ruairc's absence. Treachery abounds between friends, husbands and wives, and masters and servants, all of which helps underscore Adams' emphasis upon moral issues pertinent to the United States in the 1830s.

Adams' version of Derbforgaill depends upon David Hume, but it is more likely that Moore's version developed from Seathrún Céitinn's seventeenth-century *Foras feasa ar Éirinn*, which has this to say of her:

> Agus is ré linn Ruaidhrí Uí Chonchubhair do bheith i gceannas mar sin do chuir bean Tighearnáin Chaoich Uí Ruairc (Dearbhforgaill fá hainm dhi is fá hinghean do Mhurchadh mac Floinn rí Midhe í, agus nochar bh'í bean ríogh Midhe í, amhail adeir Cambrens) teachta ós íseal go

8 Thomas Moore, *The poetical works of Thomas Moore*, six volumes in three (Boston: Houghton, Osgood, 1878), ii, pp 107–9. **9** John Quincy Adams, *Dermot MacMorrogh, or, The conquest of Ireland* (3rd ed.; Columbus: Whiting, 1849 – University of Michigan reprint), pp v–xiii. Pages vi–xi are Hume's summary of the Norman invasion of Ireland, quoted verbatim from his *History*. I would like to thank Patrick K. Ford for alerting me to this text's existence. **10** Ibid., p. xv. **11** Adams, Canto I, stanza XXXIX, p. 30. **12** Adams, Canto I, stanza XXXV, p. 28.

> Diarmaid Mac Murchadha aga iarraidh air teacht 'n-a coinne féin da breith leis ó Thighearnán mar mhnaoi dó féin, agus adubhairt ris na teachtaibh a nochtadh do Dhiarmaid go ndeachaidh Tighearnán ar turas go huaimh Purgadóra Pádraig, agus mar sin go bhfuighbheadh seisean uain is uagneas ar í féin do bhreith leis i Laighnibh. Do bhí iomorro cumann mímhéine eatorra ré cian do bhliadhnaibh roimhe sin.
>
> And it was while Ruadhri reigned in this manner that the wife of Tighearnan Caoch O Ruairc (Dearbhforgaill was her name, and she was daughter to Murchadh Mac Floinn, king of Meath, and not wife of the king of Meath as Cambrensis says) sent messengers in secret to Diarmaid Mac Murchadha asking him to come to meet her and take her with him as his wife from Tighearnan; that Tighearnan had gone on a pilgrimage to the cave of Patrick's Purgatory, and that, therefore, he would have an opportunity of quietly carrying her with him to Leinster. There had been indeed an illicit attachment between them for many years previously.[13]

This tradition about Ua Ruairc being on a pilgrimage – which Moore also references in his song, saying that 'I look'd for the lamp which, she told me,/ Should shine when her Pilgrim return'd'[14] – was almost certainly fabricated by Céitinn; there are no references to a pilgrimage of any sort in the annals. Although international pilgrimage to Patrick's Purgatory on Lough Derg is mentioned as early as the 1140s, and may have had a presence within Ireland prior to that, it is highly unlikely that Ua Ruairc actually went.[15] Céitinn is the first to mention this purported pilgrimage, and probably does so for his own reasons. Naming Ua Ruairc as a pilgrim makes him look much better; he becomes a devoutly religious fellow – which surely appealed to Céitinn the priest – treacherously abandoned by his wife. The seventeenth-to-twentieth-century texts viewed so far, then, accuse Derbforgaill of faithlessness, and, by means of her adultery, the later Anglo-Norman invasion in 1169.

Not surprisingly, the contemporary Norman sources also portray Derbforgaill as an active party in the relationship which results in their invitation to Ireland. *The deeds of the Normans in Ireland*, an Anglo-Norman poem of the late twelfth century (also known by Goddard Orpen's title as *The song of Dermot and the earl*), portrays Derbforgaill as a simple dupe used as a pawn by Mac Murchada in order to avenge himself for some previous political injuries.

13 Seathrún Céitinn, *Foras feasa ar Éirinn*, ed. Patrick S. Dinneen, 4 vols (London: Irish Texts Society, 1902, 1908, 1914), ii, pp 318–19. **14** Moore, p. 108. **15** Peter Harbison, *Pilgrimage in Ireland* (Syracuse: Syracuse University Press, 1991), pp 55–67.

King Diarmait of Leinster,
whom this lady loved so greatly,
made a fair show of loving her,
but he did not really love her at all,
and only wanted, as far as possible,
to avenge, if he could, the great shame
which the men of Leth Cuinn had previously inflicted
on the men of Leth Moga in his territory.
King Diarmait often sent word
both by letter and by messenger
to the lady who loved him so much.
The king informed her repeatedly
that indeed she truly was
the person he loved most in the world,
and he secretly asked her many times
for her true love;
and the lady sent word to him
by private messenger
that she would do everything she was asked
by the king who was so highly esteemed;
and she asked him furthermore,
both by word of mouth and by letter,
to come for her in this way:
with all the Leinster army,
and by force and by war
to take all the land along with her.[16]

It is relevant to point out here that Derbforgaill, described in this poem in terms traditionally associated with an ingénue – naive, able to be easily manipulated – was forty-four at the time she left with Mac Murchada, and he himself was forty-two. She was certainly experienced enough to understand the political ramifications of such a move, regardless of her actual complicity or lack thereof. Additionally, her invitation to Mac Murchada in this text mirrors the later invitation Mac Murchada issues to the Anglo-Normans, particularly in her invitation to 'take all the land along with her', which clearly would not have been possible, and which picks up on, but transmutes, the issue of portable wealth she does take with her (see below). Derbforgaill, then, is used by Mac Murchada in this text, but also by the anonymous author of the text to request the nearly impossible: Ua Ruairc's land, which Mac Murchada did not get (at this point, anyway).

16 *The deeds of the Normans in Ireland*, ed. Evelyn Mullally (Dublin: Four Courts Press, 2002), lines 40–65.

In opposition to this portrayal of Derbforgaill as a political pawn, Giraldus Cambrensis, the chief chronicler of the Anglo-Norman invasion, paints Derbforgaill as fully complicit in her own abduction, and also ranks her with some of the most vilified women of all time, Helen of Troy and Cleopatra:

> she, who had long entertained a passion for Dermitius, took advantage of the absence of her husband, and allowed herself to be ravished, not against her will. As the nature of women is fickle and given to change, she thus became the prey of the spoiler by her own contrivance. For as Mark Anthony and Troy are witnesses, almost all the greatest evils in the world have arisen from women. King O'Roric being moved by this to great wrath, but more for the shame than the loss he suffered, was fully bent on revenge, and forthwith gathered the whole force of his own people and the neighbouring tribes …[17]

Notable here is the fact that Giraldus never even mentions Derbforgaill's name – she is named in a footnote by the editor of the text – nor does he even name Helen or Cleopatra. Instead, he refers to them by the men with whom or geographical locations with which they are most famously associated. Both Giraldus and the unknown author of *The deeds of the Normans in Ireland*, then, make Derbforgaill an active participant in the abduction, even if she does not herself instigate it. The Norman sources focus on her conscious decision to participate in the adulterous affair, which helps to exemplify the treachery of woman in general.

The texts discussed so far all have several things in common. First, almost all of them elide the fifteen years or so between Derbforgaill's abduction in 1152 and the expulsion of Diarmaid Mac Murchada from Ireland in 1166 and his consequent return, a year later, in 1167. Giraldus even goes so far as to say that Ua Ruairc called his troops together 'forthwith' to expel Diarmuid, but *The deeds of the Normans in Ireland*, Céitinn and Moore all telescope the intervening years in order to bring a sense of immediacy and, I think, strong emotion to the narrative. Secondly, the age of the participants, as mentioned above, is similarly elided, in order to add to the sense of romance and heighten the emotional tension around this surreptitious removal. And this emotional component is the one that is really noticeable in the contemporary Anglo-Norman and later Irish texts. The Anglo-Norman sources tend to highlight emotional sources for the politics that are taking place between Ua Ruairc and Mac Murchada: Tigernán Ua Ruairc is

17 Giraldus Cambrensis, *The conquest of Ireland*, ed. Thomas Wright, trans. Thomas Forester (London: Bohn, 1863; repr. New York: AMS, 1968), pp 184–5.

moved to revenge himself for his loss against Diarmaid because of 'shame', and Mac Murchada wants revenge against Tigernán for a long-standing grudge. This emotional component is missing from the annals, as discussed below, but it is highlighted and elaborated on by later commentators.

Anyone who has read Giraldus' *The history and topography of Ireland* knows that he, as a civilized Anglo-Norman, finds the Irish barbaric. Besides not being good Christians, they are a very violent, unpredictable and rash people, moved not by reason, but by instinct and impulse.[18] In *The conquest of Ireland*, Giraldus says that Derbforgaill had 'long entertained a passion' for Mac Murchada which overcomes her reason and makes her agree to be abducted. Ua Ruairc, according to Giraldus, is overwhelmed by 'great wrath' and 'shame' which moves him to a violent revenge. Mac Murchada is damned because he allowed himself to be seduced by Derbforgaill, thus also being ruled by passion. Essentially, this Anglo-Norman discourse serves to make the Irish less rational, driven by carnal and base instincts, and therefore practically crying out to be invaded, or at least ruled benevolently, by the much more civilized Anglo-Normans. Similarly, although *The deeds of the Normans in Ireland* claims that Mac Murchada is a good man, it only does so because he is the vehicle which allows the Normans access to Ireland; throughout the rest of the poem, it is Ireland's inherent violence and internecine warfare that are stressed.

Unsurprisingly, because they did eventually win the conflict, it is these Anglo-Norman narratives about the Norman invasion that have influenced later interpretations of the event, even for Irish commentators who are trying to reclaim Ireland's pre-eminence in the world, such as Céitinn.[19] Céitinn himself blames Derbforgaill for the invasion, and he even invents a virtuous alibi for Tigernán Ua Ruairc's absence, claiming that he is at Patrick's Purgatory in Lough Derg.[20] Moore picks up on both Giraldus' and Céitinn's clerical misogyny to castigate Derbforgaill for being fickle and faithless; her lack of loyalty to her husband causes the destruction not only of their marriage, but of a nation's entire way of life. Adams, too, sees her personal betrayal on the larger level of the state. Lady Gregory, Yeats, Joyce

18 See, in particular, the third section of Giraldus' text, particularly chs 93–107 in *The history and topography of Ireland*, trans. John J. O'Meara (New York: Penguin, 1982), pp 100–16. This attitude toward the Irish is also in evidence throughout the entire text. **19** Add to this the fact that there is no Irish literary text about the invasion on a par with Giraldus' text or the anonymous *The deeds of the Normans in Ireland*, only annal entries. **20** As seen in the quote from Céitinn's *Foras feasa* above, it is clear that he was familiar with Giraldus' work: he asserts Giraldus is wrong in calling Derbforgaill the wife of the king of Meath instead of the daughter of the king of Meath, although Giraldus could be forgiven the error: at various points in his life, Ua Ruairc was given the kingship of western Meath. It seems clear that there is a straight literary genealogy from Giraldus to Céitinn to Moore at the least; this is certainly worthy of further exploration.

and Moore all insist that one act of infidelity, often depicted as a loving relationship between Diarmaid and Derbforgaill, will cause over seven hundred years of guilt, unfulfilled romantic love and attempted revenge.

Let me now turn to the contemporary Irish sources which comment on the abduction and Derbforgaill's role in it. Essentially, what they all mention about the abduction is Derbforgaill's removal of material goods; additionally, there is no judgment made about the removal, either of person or property. The *Annals of the four masters* were compiled in the seventeenth century, based on several earlier sources, and they have this to say about Derbforgaill's abduction in 1152:

> Rugadh dna, Dearbhforgaill, inghean Murchadha Uí Mhaoileachlain, bean Tighearnan Uí Ruairc lá rí Laighean .i. Diarmaid co na crodh, 7 co na hairilleadh don turus sin, 7 ro faoi lé do réir comhairle a bráthar Mhaoileachlainn.
>
> On this occasion Dearbhforgaill, daughter of Murchadh Ua Maeleachlainn, and wife of Tighearnan Ua Ruairc, was brought away by the King of Leinster, i.e. Diarmaid, with her cattle and furniture; and he took with her according to the advice of her brother, Maeleachlainn.[21]

The English translation is fairly non-commital about Derbforgaill's responsibility, although such a removal arguably requires some forethought; it is not easy to simply show up and move cattle and possessions. When looking at the Irish, though, it's easier to see that cattle were not necessarily involved. The word *crodh* can mean 'cattle', 'herds' or 'stock', but it can equally mean 'goods', 'property', 'wealth' and, more interestingly for the later argument of this article, 'dowry'. *Airilleadh* has a secondary meaning of 'earnings', 'property', 'possessions' and 'wealth'. What is stressed in the annals, then, is that Derbforgaill, when she was removed, took a lot of wealth with her, regardless of its form, such as cattle, currency, cloth etc. Also of note is that the abduction is primarily the responsibility of Mac Murchada and Derbforgaill's brother, not Derbforgaill herself.

The Annals of Clonmacnoise, translated into English in 1627 by Conell Mageoghagan, for the year 1152 give:

> Dermott McMurrogh, king of Leinster, tooke the Lady Dervorgill, daughter of the said Morrogh O'Melaghlin, and wife of Tyernan O'Royrck, with her cattle with him, and kept her for a long space to satisfie his

21 *The Annals of the Four Masters*, ed. & trans. John O'Donovan, 2 vols (3rd ed.; Dublin: Edmund Burke, 1998), s.a. 1152.

> insatiable, carnall, and adulterous lust, shee was procured and enduced thereunto by her unadvised brother, Melaghlin for some abuses of her husband Tyernan don before.[22]

What both the Annals of Clonmacnoise and the Annals of the Four Masters stress is that Derbforgaill was taken by Diarmaid with her material wealth, and that this was her brother's idea, not her own. The Annals of Tigernach, a twelfth-century source, say of her abduction:

> [C]oruc' Diarmuid mac Murchadha ri Laigen, ben Hi-Ruairc aréicin lais a Midhi .i. Dirborgaill ingen Murchadha, cona maithius.
>
> Diarmat Mac Murchada, king of Leinster, forcibly carried off out of Meath the wife of Húa Ruairc, even Derb-forgaill, daughter of Murchad, with her wealth.[23]

About her return to Ua Ruairc in the following year, 1153, the Annals of Tigernach say: *Ingen Murchadha Húi MaelSechlainn do techt dochum Húi Ruairc arís a n-elódh o Laignib* 'the daughter of Murchad Húa Mael-Sechlainn came again to Húa Ruairc by flight from Leinster.'[24] Again, as with the Annals of the Four Masters or the Annals of Clonmacnoise, what is stressed is that Derbforgaill took material wealth with her; it is still open to question whether she brought it back with her when she returned. Finally, the *Banshenchus* notes about Derbforgaill: *(ob. 1193) mna Tigernain (ob. 1172) hUi Ruairc: qui fuit forintum onium totsiferi Hibernie meseria 7 triana híndarba Diarmada a cíbid trill iardain tar muír 7 cotagsidi Galla leis a n-Eirind*[25] 'wife of Tigernan Ua Ruairc: who was the instigator of all, almost all, the miseries of Ireland, through the expulsion of Diarmait, it happened that he journeyed over sea after a time and brought the foreigners with him to Ireland.'[26] This mixed Latin and Irish inscription is confusing, but the '*qui fuit*' absolutely refers to Tigernán as the 'instigator', and the one who expels Diarmaid – if Derbforgaill were being referred to, it would say '*quae fuit*'. If this is the case, then Tigernán, not Derbforgaill, is blamed for the Norman invasion. So if the contemporary Irish sources assign blame, they seem to blame the men involved in the action, not Derbforgaill, who is made out to be a political pawn of her agnatic relations.

22 *The Annals of Clonmacnoise*, trans. Conell Mageoghagan, ed. Denis Murphy (Dublin: Royal Society of Antiquaries of Ireland, 1896; repr. Lampeter, Llanerch, 1993), pp 199–200. **23** *The Annals of Tigernach*, trans. Whitley Stokes, 2 vols (Felinfach: Llanerch, 1993, reprint of edition published in *Revue celtique* 17 (1896), 6–33, 116–263 and 337–420; and 18 (1897), 9–59 and 150–303), ii, p. 176. **24** *The Annals of Tigernach*, ii, p. 177. **25** 'The Ban-shenchus', trans. Margaret C. Dobbs, *Revue Celtique* 48 (1931), 163–234 at 232. **26** Muireann Ní Bhrolcháin, 'The manuscript tradition of the *Banshenchas*', *Ériu* 33 (1981), 109–135 at 132.

What I would like to stress about *all* the medieval Irish sources, though, is their mention of Derbforgaill taking movable property and/or wealth with her on the occasion of her abduction. We see this in the Annals of the Four Masters, the Annals of Clonmacnoise and the Annals of Tigernach, but not in the Norman sources of Giraldus or *The deeds of the Normans in Ireland*. This is something that has been overlooked, and is bound up with Irish marriage laws. Irish and Anglo-Norman marriage laws differ quite dramatically, and one of the ways in which they differ is in the amount of property that each partner may own individually. Derbforgaill was the patron of the reconstruction of the Nuns' Church at Clonmacnoise in 1167. This surely was not inexpensive. Additionally, in 1157, at the consecration of Mellifont, Derbforgaill gave the church [*tri fichit oile uinge dór*] 7 *caileach óir ar altoir Mhairi, 7 edach ar gach naltóir do na naoi naltoraibh oile bátar isin teampall isin* '[three score ounces of gold,] and a chalice of gold on the altar of Mary, and cloth for each of the nine other altars that were in that church.'[27] Within ten years, then, Derbforgaill gave huge sums of money to the church in Ireland, and I want to link this to the constant reminder that Derbforgaill was removed with property when abducted in 1152.[28] Whenever Derbforgaill is shown as spending money, she is named in her own right; she may be called the wife of Ua Ruairc and/or the daughter of Ua MaelSechlainn, but her given name is also usually used. This implies, I think, that Derbforgaill is wealthy in her own right, and not because she shares her husband's income. In fact, this would not have been the custom of the day. Donncha Ó Corráin has argued that the most popular type of marriage that existed in Ireland until the Normans came was the *lánamnas comthincuir*, 'the marriage in which both parties, the man and the woman, jointly contribute to the marriage goods. Though these are held in common for the duration of the marriage, each of the partners retains the ultimate ownership of what he or she contributed. In Irish law there is no such thing as common marital property.'[29] This type of 'marriage of common contribution' was meant to take place between a man and a woman of equal social status, as is the case with Derbforgaill and Tigernán Ua Ruairc. Ó Corráin also makes it clear that each person in the union may have personal property besides that which is brought into the marriage, over which the individual retains control.

27 *The Annals of the Four Masters*, s.a. 1157. **28** If we take into consideration the possibility that Derbforgaill may have also been the patron of Rahan, Co. Offaly and Temple Finghin at Clonmacnoise (see Karen Overbey's article, 'Female trouble: ambivalence and anxiety at the Nuns' Church', in this volume), this simply adds to the scope of Derbforgaill's wealth. **29** Donncha Ó Corráin, 'Women in early Irish society' in M. MacCurtain and D. Ó Corráin (eds), *Women in Irish society: the historical dimension* (Westport: Greenwood, 1979), pp 1–13 at 2. Much of my discussion of the laws of Ireland will be based on Ó Corráin's elucidation of the early Irish laws governing marriage and women, as well as on the primary text that is available, *Cáin lánamna* (see Nancy

It is not necessarily unusual, then, that Derbforgaill had her own wealth to spend. What is unusual is that she brought it away with her when she was abducted or eloped. According to the marriage laws, 'anything essential to the common economy of the spouses may not be sold without consultation and common agreement and, more generally, each partner may dissolve the disadvantageous contracts entered into by the other.'[30] So whatever Derbforgaill took with her should not have been necessary to the running of the household. But what she removed was large enough to be of notice in the annals, which means that she removed, probably, a great deal of material.

While the marriage laws go on to specify that marriage partners have some freedom in disposing of their personal private property, the only instance in which it would have been acceptable to remove all personal property is if the marriage were being entirely dissolved, in the case of divorce. Divorce was available in medieval Ireland, but only under certain circumstances. A wife could divorce a husband for many reasons, as Ó Corráin enumerates: 'sterility, impotence, being a churchman (whether in holy orders or not), blabbing about the marriage bed, calumniation, wife-beating, repudiation (including taking a secondary wife), homosexuality, failure of maintenance.'[31] But it is clear that this abduction or elopement was not seen as a divorce: in 1167, the same year Mac Murchada brought a force of the Anglo-Normans to Ireland with him, according to both the Annals of the Four Masters and the Annals of Tigernach, Ua Ruairc is paid one hundred ounces of gold by Mac Murchada *il-lógh a mna* 'in compensation for his wife'.[32] Additionally, Derbforgaill returns to Ua Ruairc in 1153, although some of the annals say that she returns to her father's family first and brings

Power article below). *Cáin lánamna* (also available in a new translation by Ó Corráin in *The Field Day anthology*, v. iv (New York: New York University, 2002), pp 41–4) is an eighth century text that is preserved in a fourteenth-century manuscript. It is glossed, but the rules governing marriage seem not to have changed substantially; much of the glossing refers to changes in fine values over time. (My thanks to Charlene Eska for this information; any errors are of course mine). As of the late eleventh- and early twelfth-centuries, then, Irish law concerning marriage was still governed by a much older text, the *Cáin lánamna*. Irish kings and other high-status males seem to have participated in serial monogamy in the eleventh and twelfth centuries (if not earlier, as well), divorcing and remarrying for a variety of reasons, many of them political. See Anthony Candon, 'Power, politics and poygamy [sic]: women and marriage in late pre-Norman Ireland' in D. Bracken and D. Ó Riain-Raedel (eds), *Ireland and Europe in the twelfth century* (Dublin: Four Courts Press, 2006), pp 106–27 passim; Marie Therese Flanagan, *Irish society, Anglo-Norman settlers, Angevin kingship*, pp 91–5; and letters from Llanfranc, archbishop of Canterbury, to Guthric, king of Dublin and Toirrdelbach Ua Briain, king of Munster in the late eleventh century, found in Helen Clover and Margaret Gibson (eds & trans.), *The letters of Llanfranc, archbishop of Canterbury* (Oxford: Oxford University Press, 1979), 66–73. **30** Donnchadh Ó Corráin, 'Marriage in early Ireland' in A. Cosgrove (ed.), *Marriage in Ireland* (Dublin: College Press, 1985), pp 5–24 at 7. **31** Ibid., p. 19. **32** *Annals of Tigernach*, ii, p. 420; the *Annals of the Four Masters*, s.a. 1167 use the term *eineach*, meaning, essentially, that Ua Ruairc 'saved face' by receiving the money.

all of her things back with her.[33] Divorce may have been an available option for Derbforgaill, and may also have been for Ua Ruairc, because 'flagrant infidelity' was a just cause for divorce at the time, but neither availed themselves of this option.[34] If neither Derbforgaill nor Ua Ruairc were interested in a divorce, how might her removal, with her belongings, be explained?

There was a type of union called *lánamnas fochsail* 'union by abduction', which I suggest may apply to Derbforgaill and Mac Murchada. Most of the commentary on this type of union revolves around the children born to this type of relationship; although these laws may not apply in this instance, they illustrate that this was considered a valid, if unwelcome, form of marriage. Much of the commentary discusses what happens to the children of such a union when the wife returns to her husband, implying that the women often did return, or were returned, to their husbands. And *Cáin lánamna* 'the law of marriage', insists that: 'if the abducted woman was a *cétmuinter* "principal wife", full *éric*-fine was payable on account of her abduction.'[35] Further, there are distinctions in the amount of fine to be paid if she was taken without her permission, or with her consent. If she was taken against her wishes, then 'full honour-price was payable on her account to herself, her family and her chief. … On the other hand, if she consented to the abduction, she had no personal claim to honour-price, but this was nevertheless due to her family.'[36] Ua Ruairc was clearly paid for Derbforgaill's abduction, but the annals do not mention whether or not she also received payment.

There are two other points to be made about this abduction: the possibility that Derbforgaill was being used as a hostage, thus indicating her absolute political importance, and the apparent oddity of her childlessness in the contemporary Irish sources. The argument that Derbforgaill's political importance is much greater than previously assumed was suggested to me by Anthony Candon's article, 'Power, politics and poygamy [sic]: women and marriage in late pre-Norman Ireland'. During the course of his argument, Candon introduces Mór, wife to Conchobar Ua Máel Sechnaill, king of Meath in the mid-eleventh century, who was in all ways a remarkable woman. She witnessed a charter of her husband's, which is stunning in itself, but later, Candon argues, Mór was used as a hostage: her husband, Conchobar

33 The *Annals of Tigernach* (p. 391) say that she comes back 'by flight from Leinster'. The *Annals of the Four Masters* insist that Toirdelbach Ua Conchobair, king of Ireland, marched 'against Mac Murchadha, King of Leinster, and took away the daughter of Ua Maeleachlainn, with her cattle, from him, so that she was in the power of the men of Meath. On this occasion Tighearnan Ua Ruairc came into his house, and left him hostages' (s.a. 1153). See below for further discussion. **34** Donnchadh Ó Corráin, 'Marriage in Early Ireland', p. 19. **35** Nancy Power, 'Classes of women described in the *Senchas már*' in *Studies in early Irish law*, (Dublin: Royal Irish Academy, 1936), pp 81–108 at 90. **36** Ibid.

Ua Máel Sechnaill, offered her as a hostage to Diarmait mac Máel na mBó, king of Leinster, who had her kept in the custody of Gilla Pátraic, king of Osraige. In a scene very similar to that which happens almost one hundred years later, and involving the same families,[37] the Annals of the Four Masters report that in 1053, Diarmait mac Máel na mBó and Gilla Pátraic attack Meath, 'in revenge for the going of Mór, daughter of Congalach Ua Conchobair, to Conchobar Ua Máel Sechnaill, in violation of Gilla Pátraic, and in revenge also for the cattle which Ua Máel Sechnaill had taken from the Leinstermen.'[38] This attack is instigated because of Gilla Pátraic's realization that he has lost such a valuable hostage, Candon argues. Similarly, given the power politics at play with Derbforgaill's removal from and return to Ua Ruairc, the same argument might apply to Derbforgaill. The relationship between Ua Ruairc and Mac Murchada was almost always a fractious one, and the relationship between Ua Ruairc and his in-laws, the MaelSechlainns, frequently ran the gamut between friendly and openly hostile, depending upon what that relationship had to offer Ua Ruairc politically. If Mac Murchada had simply wanted to impoverish Ua Ruairc, he could have done so easily enough by organizing a cattle raid. But the fact that he took Derbforgaill with him as well points to her political importance.

Additionally, the abduction of Derbforgaill is an integral part of a larger whole: Toirdelbach Ua Conchobair, 'high king' of Ireland (with opposition), marched with his force into Meath, meeting there Diarmaid Mac Murchada and Muirchertach Mac Lochlainn (who later took over as 'high king' of Ireland, also with opposition). They took land from Ua Ruairc and split the kingdom of Meath between Murchad Ua MaelSechlainn and his son, MaelSechlainn.[39] Derbforgaill here becomes a political hostage to larger forces: while punishing Ua Ruairc, Mac Murchada and his allies also strengthen Derbforgaill's natal family. Removing Derbforgaill and her wealth handily accomplishes both things. Derbforgaill's political importance is further underlined by the fact that, according to the Annals of the Four Masters, Toirdelbach Ua Conchobair was the one who marched against Mac Murchada to retrieve Derbforgaill the next year, in 1153, whom he then brought to her agnatic relations in the kingdom of Meath. The situation only got more complicated, as Derbforgaill's father, Murchad Ua MaelSechlainn, also died in 1153. His son (and Derbforgaill's brother) MaelSechlainn seems to have gone to fairly extreme measures to insure his ascendancy to his father's rule: he blinded one of his nephews, Conchobar mac Domnall mac

37 Diarmait Mac Máel na mBó was Diarmaid Mac Murchada's great-grandfather; the Ua Mael Sechnaills are Derbforgaill's natal family. Conchobar was her father's great-uncle. Obviously, the political rivalry between Leinster and Meath was a long-standing one. **38** Candon, 'Power, politics and poygamy [sic]', p. 124. **39** *Annals of the Four Masters*, s.a. 1152.

Murchad Ua MaelSechlainn, although he left his other two nephews, Diarmaid and Donnchadh, alone (MaelSechlainn's brother Domnall had died in 1137).[40] This MaelSechlainn, of course, is the one who is cited as being one of the instigators for Derbforgaill's removal in the first place. The *Annals of the four masters* go on to record that *Tainig Tighearnan Ua Ruairc ina theach don chur sin, 7 ro fhágaibh braighde occa* 'Tighearnan Ua Ruairc came into his house, and left him hostages.'[41] It is unclear whether Ua Ruairc gave hostages to his brother-in-law or to Toirdelbach Ua Conchobair, but this certainly illustrates that Ua Ruairc was willing to subject himself in order to win the return of his wife, and her strategic importance is highlighted by the fact that she is being shuttled between the Kings of Leinster, Meath and Bréifne, the shuttling itself being facilitated by the 'high king' of Ireland. If not a hostage herself – and it seems likely that she was – Derbforgaill was at the very least seen as being politically important enough to require detailed consideration by several of Ireland's most important regional kings.

The fact of her considerable political importance, then, makes it even stranger that Derbforgaill is never mentioned, in any of the contemporary sources, as being the mother of any children. The *Ban-shenchus* 'the lore of women', as a number of commentators have pointed out,[42] is primarily a list of women who came of royal lineage and/or gave birth to sons who went on to become kings. Diarmaid Mac Murchada had at least seven children. As Marie Therese Flanagan details, four were legitimate by two wives: his wife Sadb had a son Donnchad and a daughter Órlaith; his wife Mór had a son Conchobar who was killed by Ruaidrí Ua Conchobair in 1170 (at Tigernán Ua Ruairc's instigation) and a daughter Aoife who went on to marry Strongbow. The other three children, two sons, Énna and Domnall Caemánach, and a daughter, Derbforgaill, do not have mothers mentioned in any of the sources.[43] The *Ban-shenchus* also says that Mac Murchada was married to a

40 *Annals of the Four Masters*, s.a. 1153. Noteworthy about Domnall's death in particular is that it came at the hands of his father, Murchad, who was resisting a revolt against his rule instigated by Domnall. See *Annals of the Four Masters*, s.a. 1137, and P. Walsh, 'The Ua Maelechlainn kings of Meath', *Irish Ecclesiastical Record* 57 (1941), 165–83 at 173. **41** Ibid. **42** See Anne Connon, 'The *Banshenchas* and the Uí Néill queens of Tara' in A.P. Smyth (ed.), *Seanchas: studies in early and medieval Irish archaeology, history and literature in honour of Francis J. Byrne* (Dublin: Four Courts Press, 2000), pp 98–108; Muireann Ní Bhrolcháin, 'The *Banshenchas* revisited' in M. O'Dowd and S. Wichert (eds), *Chattel, servant or citizen: women's status in church, state and society* (Belfast: Institute of Irish Studies, 1995), pp 70–81; and Anthony Condon, 'Power, politics and poygamy [sic]', pp 106–27. **43** Marie Therese Flanagan, *Irish society, Anglo-Norman settlers, Angevin kingship*, p. 96; *The chartularies of St. Mary's Abbey, Dublin*, ed. John T. Gilbert (London: Longman, 1884; repr. Wiesbaden: Kraus, 1965), vol. 1, pp 31–3, mention charters issued and confirmed by Derbforgaill, daughter of Mac Murchada, to St. Mary's Abbey after 1168 and likely from 1186–95. Is it possible that Derbforgaill is Mac Murchada's daughter by Derbforgaill during the year of her abduction in 1152? Although it is rather unusual for a child to inherit its parent's given name, the dates make it possible; at the time she issued and confirmed charters, Derbforgaill had several grown (and at least one married) sons,

woman named Órla, but does not mention whether or not she had children.[44] Likewise, Tigernán Ua Ruairc possibly had three children (if not more), but their mothers are never mentioned in the sources. Derbforgaill is not mentioned as being the mother of these three children in the *Ban-shenchus*, or in any of the annals. Ua Ruairc had a son, Aedh, who died in 1171,[45] another son, MaelSechlainn, who died in 1162,[46] and a daughter, Dubcoblaid, who went on to become the only wife of Ruaidrí Ua Conchobair, last 'high king' of Ireland.[47] The name MaelSechlainn is a popular one, but one that is often associated with the Ua MaelSechlainns of Meath, Derbforgaill's natal family; it is also the name of her brother who may have been involved in her abduction. It seems unlikely that this MaelSechlainn is not Derbforgaill's son, but she is never mentioned as his mother. This may be because MaelSechlainn did not live to inherit his father's kingdom; sons are often only ascribed to women in the *Ban-shenchus* who go on to become kings themselves. But it seems odd that an exception would not be made for Derbforgaill, if, as Muireann Ní Bhrolcháin argues, the metrical version of the *Ban-shenchus* was perhaps inspired by Derbforgaill herself.[48] As Karen Overbey's article in this volume, 'Female trouble: ambivalence and anxiety at the Nuns' Church', details, Derbforgaill's patronage was already extensive. It makes sense that her patronage would not be confined to architecture alone, but would extend also to the other arts. As the poet's patrons, then, a reader might expect to see the children of Ua Ruairc and Derbforgaill listed in the poem, even if they did not live to succeed to their father's kingdom.[49]

putting her, in all likelihood, in her mid-thirties to early forties, and thus at the right age to have been conceived in 1152–3. **44** 'The Ban-shenchus', trans. Dobbs, 234. **45** *Annals of the Four Masters*, s.a. 1171. **46** Ibid., s.a. 1162. **47** *Annals of Clonmacnoise*, p. 214. Ní Bhrolcháin, in 'The *Banshenchas* revisited', p. 76, states that her sources for this information are both the Annals of Clonmacnoise and the *Ban-shenchus*, but I cannot find the reference in the second text; it is possible, of course, that this Dubcoblaid was the daughter of another Ua Ruairc. Also intriguing about Dubcoblaid is that she, too, is not named as being the mother of any son, although as wife of the last 'high king' of Ireland, it might be expected that she would be mentioned. As a final note, it seems that both Dubcoblaid and the woman who was possibly her mother, Derbforgaill, were married to only one man in their lifetimes. This is unusual in an era that saw many serial marriages, and may illustrate even more strongly Derbforgaill's strategic importance. Much more work needs to be done on Dubcoblaid. **48** Ní Bhrolcháin, 'The *Banshenchas* revisited', p. 71. She notes that the poem has a eulogy to Tigernán Ua Ruairc, who was the poet's overlord: '[T]he poem ends with a tribute to Tigernán, Derborgaill and her parents. Perhaps [the poet] Gilla Mo-Dutu intended the poem to honour Derborgaill. It is, therefore, possible that she was the inspiration for this unusual metrical composition.' This would be very much in line with Overbey's assertion in her article in this volume that Derbforgaill functions as a representative for not only Bréifne, but also Meath, particularly when Meath's succession is in question, as it often was in the later twelfth century. **49** This is interesting not just for the genealogical and political implications, but also for economic ones. Derbforgaill seems to have outlived everyone in her family – she died at Mellifont in 1193 – and, since she was already an incredibly wealthy woman, it stands to reason that she inherited even

The argument that the contemporary Anglo-Norman sources and the later Irish sources have with Derbforgaill is that she is an adultress; her betrayal of her husband is seen by them all as representative of the larger betrayal of the Irish people. It is her adultery which supposedly causes the rancor between Ua Ruairc and Mac Murchada (although it simply exacerbated a long-standing feud between them), a rancor which later causes Mac Murchada's expulsion from Ireland at the hands of Ua Ruairc and his allies, and his subsequent search for allies among the Anglo-Normans. But according to Irish marriage law of the time, Derbforgaill did nothing wrong even if she did agree to the elopement (and it is not certain that she did). Additionally, Derbforgaill is more than likely a hostage, which points to her significant political importance at the time – this may even be further underscored by her abundant and evident wealth – and also perhaps her importance as a patron of the arts. This is why, I think, so little judgment is passed on Derbforgaill in the contemporary Irish annals. But for the contemporary Anglo-Norman sources, and the later Irish sources, which pick up on the conquering party's discourse, the argument that Derbforgaill is an adultress becomes an emotional focal point. It is the aspect that can simultaneously be over-sentimentalized, over-romanticized and condemned for incivility – the overly emotional Irish people overwhelmed by passion into betraying the most significant civil pact that many people make, that of marriage. This disregards Irish law and political machinations, but helps to make the argument that the Irish are barbarous because of their unusual attitude toward marriage (and the Church had long-standing issues with Irish marriage law as well).[50] In the end, then, the discourse which has come to dominate discussion about this infamous love triangle is based on a fundamental misunderstanding of the facts, laws and politics of Irish life in the twelfth century.

more wealth after the death of her husband, particularly if most of his children predeceased him. Who, then, inherited Derbforgaill's substantial wealth? Did she leave it all to the Church? Or were there grandchildren who may have inherited it? This is another avenue open for further exploration. **50** See Flanagan's *Irish society, Anglo-Norman settlers, Angevin kingship*, pp 7–55, for an overview of the Irish and English church during this time period. Also see Candon's 'Power, politics and poygamy [sic]', pp 106–10 for a concise overview of the English church's opinion about Irish marriage.

Female Trouble: Ambivalence and Anxiety at the Nuns' Church[1]

KAREN EILEEN OVERBEY

> The sense of seclusion [at the Nuns' Church] is very impressive, and suitable to its ... connexion with the repentance and retirement of the Irish Guinevere, Dervorgilla.[2]
>
> *Dervorgilla*: I brought trouble upon Ireland, as well as upon all I had to do with.[3]

Derbforgaill is trouble. The medieval literary construction of Derbforgaill makes her the source of Ireland's doom; according to Giraldus Cambrensis and the anonymous author of the Anglo-Norman poem, *The Deeds of the Normans in Ireland*,[4] her abduction by (or elopement with) Diarmaid Mac Murchada of Leinster caused the rift between Mac Murchada and Tigernán Ua Ruairc, king of Bréifne, a rupture of Ireland's internal politics that allowed foreign infiltration when Mac Murchada sought Norman allies against his rival. In these accounts – and particularly in Giraldus' *Expugnatio Hibernica* – Derbforgaill is treacherous and untrue, an Eve (or Cleopatra, or

1 Early versions of this paper were presented at the Kalamazoo Medieval Congress in May 2006 and at the Harvard Celtic Colloquium in October 2006. I am grateful for the feedback from audiences at both venues, and for insightful comments from Catherine McKenna, Rachel Moss, and the anonymous readers for *CSANAY*. It was discussions with Lahney Preston-Matto that generated my original interest in Derbforgaill, and this project has grown from and with our continued conversations and collaborations. I would also like to thank Maggie McEnchroe Williams for allowing me to reproduce her photographs of the Nuns' Church. 2 T.J. Westropp, 'A description of the ancient buildings and crosses at Clonmacnoise, King's County', *Journal of the Royal Society of Antiquaries of Ireland* 17 (1907), 277–306 at 300. 3 Augusta (Lady) Gregory, 'Dervorgilla', *Selected plays of Lady Gregory* (Washington, DC: Catholic University Press, 1983), pp 153–69 at 156. 4 This text is also known as *The Song of Dermot and the earl*, the title given by Goddard Henry Orpen in his 1892 translation. For a recent bilingual edition, see Evelyn Mullaly (ed. and trans.), *The deeds of the Normans in Ireland / La geste des engleis en Yrlande* (Dublin: Four Courts Press, 2002). 5 See Lahney Preston-Matto, 'Derbforgaill's literary heritage: can you blame her?', in this volume.

CSANA Yearbook 7: Four Courts Press, Dublin; ISSN 1649–0096; ISBN 978–1–84682–099–1

Helen) whose shameful actions expose Ireland's instability.[5] Here Derbforgaill's character is circumscribed by gender: as Giraldus put it, 'the nature of women is fickle and given to change', and the inescapability of her nature is what made Derbforgaill (and Ireland) the 'prey of the spoiler'.[6] This characterization denies Derbforgaill any real agency. She could – as Giraldus emphasizes – *choose* to be 'ravished' by Mac Murchada, but that 'choice' is merely evidence of the fickle female temperament more generally, and of the disorder that is figured in the female body.

She is certainly trouble for the twelfth century, but Derbforgaill is also trouble for scholars. According to the Annals of the Four Masters (*AFM*), the Nuns' Church at Clonmacnoise (fig. 1) was 'completed' by Derbforgaill in 1167. This is an unusual attribution of an Irish church's building to a woman, and as Jenifer Ní Ghrádaigh suggests, that atypicality has in part precluded the Nuns' Church from being seen as 'a key church for the establishment of a stylistic chronology for the Irish Romanesque', despite the apparently clear dating provided by the annals.[7] Estimations of the extent of Derbforgaill's patronage range from 'mere repair' of an existing structure, to isolated parts of the chancel arch and portal, to church furnishings and portable objects.[8] Each of these versions of Derbforgaill's role in the Nuns' Church avoids casting her as primary patron, instead justifying her donation within conventionally gendered expectations of gift giving. Most references to women's patronage in early Ireland note donations of portable objects and church furnishings – gold, cloth, liturgical vessels – 'moveable wealth' whose gifting could enhance the patron's social position.[9] Laywomen did occasionally make donations of land to religious institutions, though, as Dianne Hall notes, the legal position of women as regards land tenure meant that such grants would have required consent of their male relatives.[10] But Derbforgaill's

6 Giraldus Cambrensis, *The conquest of Ireland*, ed. Thomas Wright, trans. Thomas Forester (London: Bohn, 1863; repr. New York: AMS, 1968), pp 184–5. Thanks to Lahney Preston-Matto for discussion of this passage. **7** Jenifer Ní Ghrádaigh, '"But what exactly did she give?": Derbforgaill and the Nuns' Church at Clonmacnoise" in Heather King (ed.), *Clonmacnoise studies* 2 (Dublin: Dúchas, 2003), pp 175–207 at 175. My remarks here, regarding the perception of Derbforgaill's agency, are an attempt to tease out some of the implications of Ní Ghrádaigh's suggestion that the singularity of female patronage has made scholars suspicious of the 1167 date as referring to the building's completion. Her essay has been immensely influential in my work on this project, and I am grateful to Rachel Moss and Marie Therese Flanagan for urging me to read it carefully. **8** These three characterizations are given by Westropp, 'A description of the ancient buildings' [repairs only]; Peter Harbison, *The golden age of Irish art: the medieval achievement 600–1200* (London: Thames and Hudson, 1999) [jambs – but not voussoirs – of the chancel arch and west portal]; and Françoise Henry, *Irish art in the Romanesque period 1020–1170 AD* (Ithaca: Cornell University Press, 1970) [church furnishings]; all cited by Ní Ghrádaigh, '"But what exactly did she give?"' pp 191–2. **9** See Dianne Hall, *Women and the church in medieval Ireland, c.1140–1540* (Dublin: Four Courts Press, 2003), p. 43. One of the most frequently referenced examples for such donations, however, is Derbforgaill's own gift of gold and portable objects to Mellifont, which will be discussed below. **10** Hall, *Women and the church*, p. 43.

1. The Nuns' Church, Clonmacnoise. Photo: M. Williams

involvement in the Nuns' Church does not fit within either of these boundaries: she seems to have been the primary patron of the *architecture*, and Ní Ghrádaigh stresses that 'while Derbforgaill may well have supplied the Nuns' Church with altar cloths and furnishings, it is the structure itself that she should be remembered for.'[11] This is a role most often studied in relationship to the small number of male, royal figures whose names are associated with Romanesque building projects in Ireland: Muirchertach Ó Briain, Cormac Mac Cárthaig, Diarmaid Mac Murchada. These are also the patrons linked to major, datable monuments; as Tadhg O'Keeffe notes, 'virtually everybody else remains anonymous.'[12] Derbforgaill does not sit easily in this company. In scholarship on the Romanesque architecture of Ireland, primacy is given to those sites and figures that mark progress, that allow construction of a modernist narrative of status, power and linearity.[13] The Nuns' Church, along with Derbforgaill, has been sidelined from that narrative.[14]

11 Ní Ghrádaigh, '"But what exactly did she give?"' p. 205. 12 Tadhg O'Keeffe, *Romanesque Ireland* (Dublin: Four Courts Press, 2003), p. 232. 13 My thoughts here have been shaped in large part by the work of O'Keeffe, in particular his articulation of the emphasis on ecclesiastical reform in the scholarship of the Romanesque Ireland; see *Romanesque Ireland*, pp 21–60. 14 There is for me an intriguing resonance here with the perception of higher- and lower-status craft activities in

Both church and patron, I want to argue here, have been inserted into another 'history', one told through juxtaposition and collapse. In the medieval accounts of Derbforgaill, the time between her abduction by Mac Murchada and the entry of the Normans into Ireland is elided, setting Derbforgaill's 'fickleness' up against the invasion as cause-and-effect.[15] While this places her in what might seem a specific historical moment, the result is rather to de-historicize Derbforgaill, mythologizing her as a marker of the transition from Gaelic to Norman Ireland. This medieval literary destabilization of Derbforgaill's chronology has a parallel in modern architectural scholarship – the excerpt from the antiquarian T.J. Westropp's description with which this essay opens is one example of the art historical accounts that allow the Nuns' Church and the Norman invasion to lie uncomfortably close to each other, with just the slimmest blade of scholarly propriety between them. Westropp associates – albeit very insubstantially – the Nuns' Church with Derbforgaill's supposed repentance for her role in Ireland's loss of sovereignty, casting her patronage as an act of personal redemption. I do not mean to suggest that modern historians of the Nuns' Church intended, as Giraldus did, to construct Derbforgaill's culpability for the invasion; the juxtapositions in art historical scholarship are, on the surface, more benign than that, and their effects more subtle. My objective is rather to explore some of the history of those juxtapositions, and their implications for the reception of the church and the patron.

THE POLITICS OF PATRONAGE

Before addressing that history, however, I want to expand some of what has been collapsed: Derbforgaill's patronage before, and besides, the Nuns' Church. By 1167, Derbforgaill had already been active as a patron of art and architecture for at least a decade, benefaction that should be understood as politically rather than penitentially motivated, and as representative of Derbforgaill's role as a royal woman, wife and daughter, rather than as the 'Irish Guinevere'.

Ireland. Ní Ghrádaigh, in a recent essay, argues that 'as long as modern scholars think only in terms of masons and stone, we are overlooking a whole team of other craftsmen who were equally active in the production of the final building, wooden and metal fitting included'; Jenifer Ní Ghrádaigh, 'A legal perspective on the *saer* and workshop practice in pre-Norman Ireland' in Rachel Moss (ed.), *Making and meaning in Insular art* (Dublin: Four Courts Press, 2007), pp 110–25 at 123. Ní Ghrádaigh translates and discusses a text concerned with the refection of various types of craftsmen, and notes that the text distinguishes crafts that involved erection/construction from those that did not (p. 114). A similar hierarchy in our perception of patronage seems to presuppose women's exclusion from erection/construction of buildings; this is a resonance that, I think, requires more attention. **15** On that elision see Preston-Matto, this volume.

Derbforgaill's earliest recorded donation is to Mellifont, established in 1142 as the first Cistercian house in Ireland; the foundation was initiated by St Malachy, on lands granted by Donnchad Ua Cergaill, king of Airgialla. At the 1157 consecration, Derbforgaill gave sixty ounces of gold, a gold chalice for the altar of Mary and nine altar cloths (*AFM*). Mellifont was the largest church yet built in Ireland, and the grand ceremony was attended by church and state officials including the papal legate, archbishops of Armagh, Dublin and Tuam, eighteen bishops, high king Muirchertach Mac Lochlainn, and four other kings including Derbforgaill's husband, Tigernán Ua Ruairc of Bréifne. As Marie Therese Flanagan has argued, the annals record the attending dignitaries in a hierarchy of power and their donations in a graduated scale, reflecting their relative status.[16] Derbforgaill's name and her gifts are listed along with those of the provincial kings – she is the wife of Ua Ruairc, but also the daughter of Murchadh Ua MaelSechlainn, the king of Meath who had died four years earlier in 1153. On his death, his son MaelSechlainn Ua MaelSechlainn assumed the kingship, but was poisoned two years later, and from 1155 to 1160 the title passed several times between Murchadh's nephews Donnchad and Diarmaid. Donnchad held power briefly in 1157, but, at the time of the Mellifont consecration, was excommunicated and deposed, and Diarmaid installed in his place – another brief kingship, lasting only into 1158.[17]

It is possible that Derbforgaill's presence and donation at Mellifont functioned to represent the Meath dynasty as securely as possible in the face of that dynastic disturbance, a purpose strengthened if the donation were drawn from Derbforgaill's own wealth rather than that of her husband Ua Ruairc; that may have been the case, especially as Derbforgaill is mentioned by name in the annals. Ní Ghrádaigh has proposed something similar for the Nuns' Church, regarding Derbforgaill's patronage there as a mark of Ua MaelSechlainn family interest,[18] and Lahney Preston-Matto's discussion of pre-Norman Irish marriage customs makes clear that wives of Derbforgaill's status would have retained control over personal, family wealth.[19] But the Mellifont ceremony was more than a religious consecration: it was also the first public endorsement of Mac Lochlainn as high king. The occasion probably served as much to officially recognize his status as it did to dedicate the altar, and Derbforgaill's donation underscores this dual function. As

16 Marie Therese Flanagan, *Irish royal charters: texts and contexts* (Oxford: Oxford University Press, 2005), p. 117. **17** On the tangled succession, see Paul Walsh, 'The Ua Maelechlainn kings of Meath', *Irish Ecclesiastical Record* 57 (1941), 165–83. Walsh puts Donnchad's excommunication at 'a synod held in connexion with the consecration of the church of Mellifont' (176) – if the events were indeed synchronous, the disruptions in the Ua MaelSechlainn family would have been even more evident at the ceremony. **18** Ní Ghrádaigh, '"But what exactly did she give?"' p. 178. **19** Preston-Matto, this volume.

2. West portal of the Nuns' Church. Photo: M. Williams

representative of both Meath and Bréifne, Derbforgaill's contribution to Mellifont endorsed Mac Lochlainn's rule and demonstrated secular allegiance and hierarchy *at least* as much as piety. Derbforgaill's gift has been seen as exemplary of women's religious patronage in medieval Ireland, patronage that functioned to elevate the (female) giver's social status through pious charity.[20] Derbforgaill's donation to Mellifont, however, might be seen as functioning for her family rather than for her self, and as *demonstrating* rather than enhancing status: her patronage attests to the standing of the Ua MaelSechlainn family at this public ceremony, and is a display of wealth, virtue and authority on a par with those of the other provincial dynasties.

Viewing Derbforgaill's contribution in this political light also allows a re-examination of the scope of her architectural patronage. While the annals record Derbforgaill's 'completion' of the Nuns' Church in 1167, it was an enterprise in which her family had been involved over a longer period. In 1144, her father, the king of Meath, granted the 'church of the nuns' at Clonmacnoise to the Arroasian community at Clonard. Derbforgaill's sister Agnes (d. 1196) was the first abbess of Clonard, itself founded by the Ua MaelSechlainn family.[21] As at Mellifont, then, we should understand Derbforgaill's patronage of the Nuns' Church at Clonmacnoise as part of political, if not dynastic, aspirations.

20 See above, n. 8. **21** Hall, *Women and the church*, p. 60.

3. Detail of the west portal of the Nuns' Church. Photo: K. Overbey

The renovations of the Nuns' Church in the mid-twelfth century enlarged an early-eleventh-century structure (likely the one destroyed by fire in 1082, as described in *AFM*) and added the west portal and chancel arch decorated in the Romanesque style. The four-ordered portal (fig. 2) includes chevrons, spiral cones and roll mouldings with stylized animal heads on the voussoirs (fig. 3). This decorative style – of which the Nun's Church is one of the earliest examples in Meath[22] – has long been associated, formally, with a Norman aesthetic, and ideologically, with ecclesiastical reform. The latter association has contributed to an understanding of twelfth-century church patronage as primarily religiously motivated, and may to some degree underlie – though quite tenuously – the association of the Nun's Church with penitence.

Although Romanesque forms and motifs could, especially in the early years of the twelfth century, 'articulate ideas raised by or germane to the issue of reform',[23] by the time the Nuns' Church was renovated, Romanesque was neither innovative in Ireland nor a 'metaphor for reform.'[24] The kinds of renovations made at sites like the Nun's Church – the enlargement of the nave and the addition of a decorated chancel arch – were not liturgically

22 As O'Keeffe outlines, it was not until the 1160s that Romanesque forms were utilized in Meath, although they appear in Munster in the 1120s and Leinster in the 1140s; *Romanesque Ireland*, p. 252. **23** Ibid., p. 283. **24** Ibid., p. 282.

motivated; that is, structural or spatial changes were not required for reforms to the liturgy or devotional practices. O'Keeffe argues that the introduction of the style in Ireland through Munster sites such as Killaloe, Ardfert and, especially, Cashel tied the Romanesque more to secular politics and status than to religious reform. Cormac's Chapel at Cashel, he writes, 'was a powerful and widely recognized demonstration of the political potency of church patronage, and Romanesque details achieved popularity through being associated with it.'[25] Church renovations, and especially the additions of Romanesque forms, were driven by a desire for patronage to visually resonate with political aspirations. O'Keeffe proposes that patrons who emulated the designs of Cashel (as Diarmaid Mac Murchada did at his royal chapel at Ferns) did so with the intention of equating political power with a specific visual vocabulary – a vocabulary whose syntax was most potently local rather than universal or Norman.[26] If there was an ideological force behind Derbforgaill's renovation of the Nuns' Church, there is no reason to cast that motivation as penitential or remorseful. It is much more appropriate that her patronage be seen as part of the political activity of a regional ruling family. Rather than solely expressing piety, we can view Derbforgaill's patronage of the Nun's Church as a demonstration of progressive political leanings in accord with other provincial Irish powers, male or female. And as such it might be viewed not as a singular and unusual instance of female architectural patronage, but as one among several possible sites of Derbforgaill's interest.

While nothing is documented about the patronage of Rahan, Co. Offaly, for example, the chevron-decorated oculus and some details on the chancel arch have parallels at the Nuns' Church, and both are attributed to the same sculptor.[27] A capital and voussoir from the south doorway of Temple Finghin at Clonmacnoise also show the same hand as some of the work at the Nuns' Church,[28] and Ní Ghrádaigh has recently argued that Temple Finghin, the Nuns' Church and Rahan were the products of a 'genuine workshop'.[29] Ní Ghrádaigh cautions that there is very little information available about craftsmen in medieval Ireland:

> Despite knowing the date and patron [of the Nuns' Church], we have no idea who the craftsmen involved were, let alone how many of them there were, how much they might have charged for their work, and

25 Tadhg O'Keeffe, 'Wheels of words, networks of knowledge: Romanesque scholarship and Cormac's Chapel' in Damian Bracken and Dagmar Ó Riain-Raedel (eds), *Ireland and Europe in the twelfth century: reform and renewal* (Dublin: Four Courts Press, 2006), pp 257–69 at 265. **26** Ibid. **27** Ní Ghrádaigh, 'A legal perspective', p. 110. **28** Jenifer Ní Ghrádaigh, 'Temple Finghin, and two unusual voussoirs from Clonmacnoise', *Archaeology Ireland* 19:3 (2005), 26–31. **29** Ní Ghrádaigh, 'A legal perspective', p. 124.

> whether they were attached in some manner to the monastery itself, or habitually worked for Derbforgaill and her family.[30]

Although the connection cannot be proven, the possibility that Derbforgaill and her family may have regularly employed a workshop of decorative sculptors could indicate a greater scope to her patronage than what is made visible by the annals. Rahan was within the diocese of Meath, and so if Derbforgaill was involved in that project it may have been, like the renovations of the Nuns' Church, as a representative of Ua MaelSechlainn interests. But she may also have acted as a royal patron in Bréifne. O'Keeffe compares the four-ordered portal from Trinity Island, Lough Oughter,[31] to the chancel arch at the Nuns' Church; the two correspond in a 'whole spectrum of sculptural detail' including false columns, stylized animal heads, Urnes-style ornament, and saw-toothed chevrons whose intersections form hollow lozenges.[32] The Trinity Island portal is the only extant significant work of the period from Bréifne, Ua Ruairc's kingdom, and O'Keeffe suggests it may have been through Derbforgaill that the same workshop was employed there as at Clonmacnoise.[33] It is possible – though the works themselves are lost to us – that the Trinity Island portal was part of a larger program of royal patronage in Bréifne, perhaps sponsored or overseen by Derbforgaill, drawing on her connections with Meath artists. This would suggest even more strongly that Derbforgaill's patronage was political, and like her donation to Mellifont in 1157, would indicate her awareness of her own position across dynastic boundaries.

Additionally, if Derbforgaill had a hand in the church at Rahan, then we must also assume that, like Mac Murchada at his chapel at Ferns, she was attentive to the ideological syntax of the forms – Rahan's plan and cross-section are derived from those of Cashel,[34] and so should be seen as part of what O'Keeffe has called the 'knowledge network' of 'cultural and political points of reference' for twelfth-century readers of architecture.[35] In both Meath and Bréifne, Derbforgaill was likely active as a royal patron, ensuring that her families' lands – despite the absence of prolific and highly visible architectural patrons like the Ó Conchobhair kings of Connacht or Mac Murchada in Leinster – were situated within the network of knowledge.

30 Ibid., p. 110. **31** The portal was removed from Trinity Island and reinstalled at Kilmore Cathedral in the mid-1800s. See O. Davies, 'The churches of county Cavan', *Journal of the Royal Society of Antiquaries of Ireland* (1948), 73–118; cited by O'Keeffe, *Romanesque Ireland*, p. 267 n. 62. **32** Ibid., pp 263–8. **33** Ibid., p. 267. **34** See Ní Ghrádaigh, 'A legal perspective', p. 124 and O'Keeffe, *Romanesque Ireland*, p. 88.

> [Y]ou can … reach the Nun's Church by walking … down a lane flecked with buttercups and daisies. It was completed in 1167 by Devorguilla, daughter of the King of Meath, as an offering of remorse: though married to Tiernan O'Rourke, Devorguilla deserted him for Dermot MacMurrough, an act that may have hastened the Norman invasion of Ireland. She repented for four decades before her death in 1193.[36]

> Clonmacnoise, the most beautiful and important of Ireland's monastic sites, on a bend of the Shannon, is best approached from the river … Its riches and reputation attracted Viking invaders who plundered it repeatedly. In 1170, Darbforgaill (Dervorgilla), who was abducted from her husband by Diarmait MacMurchada (Dermot MacMurrough), retired here in penance. (The Normans invaded Ireland when Dermot MacMurrough called in Strongbow to support him against his rivals, including Dervorgilla's angry husband!)[37]

Derbforgaill retired to Mellifont, the site of her earliest recorded patronage, in 1186 and died there in 1193, probably in her late eighties. She did not, as the second of these two quotes – from a travel guide for golfers – claims, retire to the Nuns' Church. But in the popular imagination, Derbforgaill dies at Clonmacnoise, filled with regret. The politics of Derbforgaill's patronage has been clouded by this tradition, that she rebuilt the Nuns' Church as penance for her role – willing or not – in the provincial rivalries that precipitated the invasion. Of course, neither the travel guide nor the *New York Times* article (the first of the quotes above) makes an explicit connection between the Nuns' Church and the invasion; Derbforgaill's motivations for patronage are 'remorse' and 'penance', respectively, which are most directly connected to her desertion/abduction. But each text links *that* event to the entry of the Normans, reproducing a metanarrative of female guilt and the loss of land; the golfers' guide even sandwiches Derbforgaill between two invasions. We might dismiss these examples as innocuous misinformation, melodramatic fantasy or titillating tourist rhetoric. We might dismiss them, that is, were it not for a similarly – albeit more subtly – persistent pathos in art historical scholarship: the association of Derbforgaill's patronage and the Norman invasion seems to have originated with the early studies of the Nuns' Church.

Although a drawing of the Nun's Church by the topographical artist Jonas Blaymires was included in the 1739 edition of Ware's *Antiquities of*

35 O'Keeffe, 'Wheels of words', p. 266. 36 Thomas Mallon, 'Here lie the High Kings of Ireland', *New York Times*, 17 Nov. 1985. 37 Roisin McAuley, *Emerald greens: the essential guide to golf vacations in Ireland* (Northampton, MA: Interlink Publishing Group, 2000), p. 130.

Ireland, the church was left out of George Petrie's *Ecclesiastical architecture of Ireland* (1845) – perhaps because of the state of the ruins (the last of the chancel arch had fallen since the time of Blaymires' sketch), or perhaps because the European forms did not fit within Petrie's framework for the development of Insular styles. It was only with the 1865 renovation of the church by the Kilkenny Archaeological Society that the building garnered scholarly interest.[38] James Graves, the antiquarian supervising that renovation, published the Society's report of repairs, and mentions the patron only in a footnote, quoting the Annals of the Four Masters, but adding that Derbforgaill was the 'paramour of Dermod Mac Murrough, King of Leinster, and is famous as the indirect cause of the Anglo-Norman conquest of Ireland.'[39] Graves' account is anything but sensationalizing – his focus was on a careful reconstruction of the medieval fabric of the building, based on artifactual evidence and documentary research, a methodology Ní Ghrádaigh has characterized as 'balanced' and 'enlightened.'[40] Perhaps in enhancing the annalistic entry, Graves meant to provide a more complete context for the church; perhaps he meant to create a sense of excitement or exoticism around the newly restored building. Nevertheless, Graves sets a scholarly precedent, and boosts Derbforgaill's notoriety by his 'indirect' association of the church and the invasion.[41]

Robert Rolt Brash, in *The ecclesiastical architecture of Ireland* (1875), devotes a long entry to Clonmacnoise, including the round tower, the cathedral, Temple Ciaran, Temple Finghin, three smaller buildings, the sculptured crosses and the Nuns' Church. Brash's is the first detailed description of the church, which he affirms as 'one of the few early ecclesiastical buildings in Ireland the date of which can be accurately fixed,' as 'the present remains undoubtedly belong to the church erected by Dervorgilla, the daughter of Murchadh O'Melachlain, in AD 1167, as we find recorded in the Annals of the Four Masters.'[42] Here Brash quotes the annals and follows with the 1082 entry noting that the earlier church on the site was destroyed by fire. He uses

38 Ní Ghrádaigh, '"But what exactly did she give?"' pp 180–1. Blaymires' drawing of the Nun's Church, which Ní Ghrádaigh reproduces as her Ill. 3, was not included in later editions of Ware; cf. the 1764 edition printed in Dublin by Robert Bell. It is not clear why this image was dropped from the later editions, but may indicate a lack of sustained interest in the site in the eighteenth century. **39** James Graves, 'Proceedings', *Journal of the Royal Society of Antiquaries of Ireland* 3 (1864–5), 367–70; quoted in Ní Ghrádaigh, '"But what exactly did she give?"' p. 191. **40** Jenifer Ní Ghrádaigh, '"My dear Pickwick": the early sketchbooks of James Graves, and his development as an antiquarian', *Ossory, Laois and Leinster* 2 (2006), 96–122 at 98 and 101. **41** The source of Graves' information about Derbforgaill's role in the invasion is not noted, but may have been based on a combination of literary and oral traditions. Although Orpen's translation of *The song of Dermot and the earl* did not appear until 1892, other excerpts and reproductions, such as M. Victor Le Clerc's 1837 edition, would have been familiar to nineteenth-century scholars. **42** Robert Rolt Brash, *The ecclesiastical architecture of Ireland* (London: Simpkin, and Marshall, 1875), p. 79.

this documentary evidence to assess the chronology of the Nuns' Church and to set the architectural sculpture into the context of the Romanesque in France and England.[43] There is no mention of Derbforgaill's abduction/ elopement, nor of her connection to the Norman invasion, nor of her motivations for patronage – penitential or otherwise.

Brash frames his study of Romanesque architecture in Ireland as a corrective to Petrie: he sets out to re-date many of the buildings that Petrie had assigned to the eighth and ninth centuries, including Timahoe, Killaloe and Rahan, and he adds others, such as the Nuns' Church, that Petrie had omitted. His method is to survey early sources, such as Archdall's *Monasticon* and Ware's *Antiquities*, along with medieval annals, and to make comparisons with Romanesque examples in France, England and Normandy. Brash is concerned primarily with dating and with affirming Irish architectural sites as places of prestige. He gathers and discusses annalistic references to each church, establishing the antiquity of locations and foundations and their importance: Ardfert, for example, 'was once a town of historic importance, and the seat of a bishopric;' for Donoughmore, 'we have scarcely any information as to its history in times past [but] that it was a church of some importance we can judge from the care bestowed on its erection … There can be no doubt that this was the monastery of which [St.] Farannan was abbot … it was a very ancient territorial denomination … [with] eminent ecclesiastics.'[44] Brash is careful to show that he is a thorough historian, noting for instance that the four excerpts he reproduces from AFM regarding Freshford and its founder St Lachtin are 'all the historic references I have been able to find respecting this place.'[45] Of Clonmacnoise, he writes that

> There is perhaps no locality in Ireland so interesting in an archaeological point of view … its early history for several centuries being interwoven with the civil and religious affairs of the whole island … Not only ecclesiastics, but men of the highest rank, from France, Belgium and Germany, sought its peaceful retreat, and drank from its fountains of pure intellectual truth. The sons of the nobility and heirs apparent of the provincial kings were sent here to be educated. It produced men of great attainments and learning, if we consider the age in which they lived; many notices of such are scattered through our annals.[46]

43 Brash dates the 'enrichments of the arch-members of the doorway and chancel-ope' to the 1167 renovation, but suggests that the capitals are 'peculiarly Irish' and of an earlier date; *Ecclesiastical architecture*, p. 79. On the consequences of this disjunction for the reception of the Nuns' Church and of Derbforgaill's patronage, see Ní Ghrádaigh, '"But what exactly did she give?"' pp 191–2. **44** Brash, *Ecclesiastical architecture*, pp 38 and 54. **45** Ibid., p. 101. **46** Ibid., p. 61.

It is not surprising, given Brash's focus on prestige and attention to 'documentary evidence' that he does not link the Norman invasion to the Nuns' Church and its patron. He cites Graves, and so must have been aware of that author's association of Derbforgaill and the conquest; perhaps that juxtaposition would have diluted the image of Clonmacnoise as a 'peaceful retreat.' But the omission also underscores Brash's skepticism of the role of oral, folkloric and 'popular' histories in antiquarian scholarship. He devotes the last two chapters of *Ecclesiastical architecture* to a discussion of the 'many curious legends [that] are extant among the peasantry' regarding Gobhan Saor, the 'reputed builder of not only our Round Towers, but of most of our ancient churches and castles.'[47] Petrie had written about the popular tradition in 1845, and suggested that Gobhan was an historical figure of the early seventh century, responsible for the erection of the towers at, among other locations, Kilmacduagh and Glendalough.[48] Brash counters this by surveying the evidence for the practices and status of craftsmen in medieval Irish texts, and by arguing that the traditions of Gobhan stemmed from the myths of the Tuatha De Danann.[49] For Brash, folklore and archaeology needed to maintain an appropriate distance.

The relative status of 'documentary evidence' and 'popular tradition' remained debatable, however, as is indicated by Westropp's 1907 account, which I now quote at greater length:

> The Nun's Church – This beautiful little oratory, with its richly carved arches rising against the fine background of trees, is no less fascinating to the artist than to the antiquary. The sense of seclusion is very impressive, and suitable to its former object and its connexion with the repentance and retirement of the Irish Guinevere, Dervorgilla … Little did the penitent, thinking only of her own sins, realize that, in addition, the sins of chiefs, churchmen, and warriors, the anarchy following the Norman wars, the feebleness of disunion, and all their results, would be heaped on her head by later historians.
>
> 'The years have rolled into the centuries,
> But hers will ever be a name of scorn.'[50]

Westropp seems aware of a gap between Derbforgaill's rebuilding project and the Norman invasion of Ireland – he tempers his rather gothic fantasy of the Nuns' Church ever so slightly, admitting that Derbforgaill could hardly have foreseen, in 1167, the consequences of Mac Murchada's involvement with

47 Ibid., pp 164 and 155. **48** George Petrie, *The ecclesiastical architecture of Ireland: an essay on the origins of round towers in Ireland* (Dublin: Hodges and Smith, 1845), pp 383–4. **49** Brash, *Ecclesiastical architecture*, pp 157–62. **50** Westropp, 'A description of the ancient buildings', pp 300–1.

English forces. Westropp was a scholar of folklore, and used oral histories to explain place-name derivations, landscape characteristics and, frequently, architectural or sculptural features, such as the bullaun stones associated with several portal tomb sites, which he suggests were used to make offerings to the sídhe.[51] But at the Nuns' Church, Westropp does not apply the legend of Derbforgaill to interpretation or explanation; he collects, but does not analyze – and the problematic gap is made invisible under the protective cover of a poetic juxtaposition.

This association has been commodified, and is treated as a kind of documentary evidence in contemporary art historical scholarship. Peter Harbison opens his discussion of the Nuns' Church, for example, with 'the Annals of the Four Masters reported that, in 1167, Dearbhforgaill, otherwise Dervorgilla, the lady abducted (perhaps willingly) by Diarmaid McMurrough, finished the Nuns' Church at Clonmacnoise …'[52] And the caption for the photograph of the church in Eamonn Kelly's book on sheela-na-gigs reads:

> Romanesque church known as the Nun's Chapel, Clonmacnois, Co. Offaly. The chapel was built by Dervorgilla, wife of Tiernan O'Rourke. Her elopement with Dermot Mac Murrough, King of Leinster, led to a war and the banishment of Mac Murrough. The Leinster king returned with Norman allies, and so began the Norman invasion of Ireland. The Nun's Chapel was completed in 1167, two years before the invasion.[53]

Even O'Keeffe – whose *Romanesque Ireland* (2003) evaluates the field's historiography and proposes ways of reading Irish architecture as driven by ideology rather than solely by style – relies on the story to provide context. Between his discussion of the church's patronage and its architectural features, he admits that Derbforgaill's 'claim to fame, of course, is that … Diarmait Mac Murchada "abducted" her from her husband Tigernán Ó Ruairc of Breifne, an action of his which contributed greatly to his subsequent exile and to the eventual invasion of the Anglo-Normans.'[54] None of these accounts provide either a source or a justification for the association of Derbforgaill's abduction with the Norman invasion; what was likely constructed by Giraldus Cambrensis has become naturalized, and apparently part of a neutral, received tradition. Françoise Henry, in *Irish art in the Romanesque period* (1970), came closest to troubling the correspondence when she characterized Derbforgaill's abduction as 'an incident which has

51 See T.J. Westropp, 'A folklore survey of County Clare', *Folklore* 21–5 (1910–16). **52** Harbison, *The golden age of Irish art*, p. 345. The annals, to clarify, do not mention Mac Murchada or the abduction at this entry. **53** Eamonn P. Kelly, *Sheela-na-gigs: origins and functions* (Dublin: Country House, 1996), p. 20, plate 8. **54** O'Keeffe, *Romanesque Ireland*, p. 262.

been magnified all out of proportion.' But Henry goes on to suggest that '[o]ne may wonder' if the compensation paid by Mac Murchada to Ua Ruairc for the abduction 'was used by the repentant Dervorgilla in the work of completion of the Nuns' Church at Clonmacnoise.'[55] Less lurid by far than Westropp – but Henry still discursively locates the Nuns' Church within a narrative of invasion.

To assess the tenacity of this juxtaposition, I want to return to Westropp, or at least to 1907, the same year in which Lady Gregory's *Dervorgilla: an Irish tragedy play* appeared. Like Westropp's description, Gregory's text surely draws from earlier traditions, both textual and oral, about Derbforgaill's guilt and remorse. Gregory's Derbforgaill, cloistered in penitence at Mellifont, wails: 'It was I brought them [the English] in … by my own sin and the wars that were stirred up for my sake … I brought trouble upon Ireland, as well as upon all I had to do with.' She professes love for Mac Murchada, and admits her active choice of him over her husband, despite her knowledge that 'O'Rourke was a good man, and a brave man, and a kinder man than Diarmuid …'[56] Gregory's play – and specifically her Derbforgaill – resonates with the kind of patriotism expressed a decade later by Yeats in *The dreaming of the bones*, a patriotism in which Irish traitors are more deeply dangerous than the invading English. But it is also rooted in a post-Famine socio-psychological 'embourgoisement' (to use Joel Hollander's term) in which women's ethical responsibility for the domestic sphere was a microcosm of the Irish nation.[57] Hollander characterizes this 'nationalist ideal of a new domesticity'[58] as valorizing strong women, but demanding from them virtuousness and chastity – as exemplified by the pictorial representations of a warrior-like Erin popularized in the press at the end of the nineteenth century. Hollander describes Erin's 'statuesque form' and 'flowing white and green garments' which 'presuppose a virtuousness and chastity that renders her untouchable and thus almost asexual.'[59] The Derbforgaills of the Abbey Theater are the antithesis of this Erin: weak, wailing and wanton, they are driven by passion to betray home, family and country. That unchaste women were dangerous to Ireland's political economy was underscored by – if not in part constructed through – Parnell's affair with Kitty O'Shea in the 1880s: Parnell's political life, and the unity of the Irish Parliamentary Party, were ruined in the scandal.

55 Françoise Henry, *Irish art of the Romanesque period*, p. 24. **56** Gregory, 'Dervorgilla', pp 156 and 166. **57** Joel A. Hollander, '"Beauty and the beast": depiction of Irish female types during the era of Parnell, *c.*1880–1891' in Lawrence W. McBride (ed.), *Images, icons and the Irish nationalist imagination* (Dublin: Four Courts Press, 1999), pp 53–72 at 54. Here Hollander is discussing Joanna Bourke's thesis regarding the dichotomous depictions of Erin and Madame Anastasie; see Joanna Bourke, '"The best of all home rulers": the economic power of women in Ireland, 1880–1914', *Irish Economic and Social History* 18 (1991), 24–37. **58** Hollander, '"Beauty and the beast"', p. 54.

The juxtapositions of abduction and invasion that serve as 'context' in art historical scholarship seem devoid of these political associations; they appear to recite facts so common as to require no authorship. In *Ulysses*, Joyce draws Derbforgaill and O'Shea together, in another juxtaposition, as part of the history lesson related to Stephen Dedalus by Mr Deasy in the 'Nestor' episode:

> A woman brought sin into the world. For a woman who was no better than she should be, Helen, the runaway wife of Menelaus, ten years the Greeks made war on Troy. A faithless wife first brought strangers to our shore here, MacMurrough's wife and her leman, O'Rourke, prince of Breffni. A woman too brought Parnell low. Many errors, many failures, but the one sin.[60]

Joyce's Deasy is a twentieth-century Giraldus Cambrensis, updating the litany of troubling women. But the context of this speech is one in which authority, and especially the rigidity of historical memory, is called into question.[61] Deasy's lesson is not only flawed in its 'facts' – the reversal of Mac Murchada and Ua Ruairc's roles – but is destructive and distorting in its implications. Joyce's critique (which is visible in Deasy's pompous nature, and perhaps most potently, in his offensive remark about Jews in Ireland) of a simultaneously aggregative and reductive metanarrative highlights the ease with which such associations are recited and reproduced, especially – though perhaps most dangerously – in the context of a nation re-imagining its origins. The traditions of Derbforgaill in art historical scholarship only *appear* neutral, and only if their 'authority' is ignored. Their articulations in both the twelfth and the twentieth centuries are ideological, and bound up with gendered constructions of loss, guilt, and authenticity.

OPENINGS AND (DIS)CLOSURES

In *The dreaming of the bones*, Yeats imagines Derbforgaill as desiccated, withered. Even as they are locked into eternal erotic longing, Diarmaid only ever sees her as an osseous corpse, buried in dry earth. Yeats' Derbforgaill thus

59 Ibid., p. 66. Hollander here describes John D. Reigh's illustration 'Freedom of the press', in *United Ireland*, 8 October 1887, which is reproduced as his fig. 3.4 on p. 65. **60** James Joyce, *Ulysses*, ed. Danis Rose (London: Picador, 1997), p. 35. **61** See for example Hélène Cixous, 'Joyce: the (r)use of writing', in Derek Attridge and Daniel Ferrer (eds), *Post-structuralist Joyce: essays from the French* (Cambridge: Cambridge University Press, 1984), pp 15–30, and John Rickard, 'Stephen Dedalus among schoolchildren: the schoolroom and the riddle of authority in *Ulysses*', *Studies in the Literary Imagination* 30:2 (1997), 17–36.

seems an iteration of nineteenth-century antiquarian responses to sheela-na-gigs, the carvings of naked females posed to display their genitals, about one hundred of which are recorded from medieval Ireland. Sheela-na-gigs were first given scholarly attention in the 1840s in published sketches and archaeological accounts. As Catherine Karkov has argued, the antiquarians' texts and images were 'overt act[s] of interpretation': some believed the sculptures had originally functioned as grave markers, and so associated their features with death and destruction – others granted the figures a spectral eroticism.[62] John Windele's drawing of the Rochestown, Co. Tipperary sheela-na-gig, for example, shows a longhaired, full-breasted woman seemingly masturbating with her eyes closed, a voyeuristic fantasy that Karkov notes resembles no extant sheela.[63] In their displays of both decay and sexuality, sheela-na-gigs were regarded as dangerous, dangerous enough to occasionally be buried or thrown into rivers by nineteenth-century Irish churchmen.[64]

I do not mean to imply that Yeats consciously created a Derbforgaill based on antiquarian accounts of sheela-na-gigs, but rather to suggest another strand in the net of associations in which the figure of Derbforgaill has been caught – associations that, although resistant to cohesive readings, persist. In the carvings of the chancel arch at the Nun's Church, defined inside a pelleted diamond motif, is a small nude figure, its hips upended to expose a genital or anal opening (fig. 4). It was Jørgen Andersen in his seminal (though now seriously outdated) 1977 book, *The witch on the wall: medieval erotic sculpture in the British Isles*, who identified the Clonmacnoise figure as the first sheela-na-gig in Ireland,[65] a distinction promoted more recently by Lisa Bitel. In *Land of women*, Bitel writes that the motif 'probably reached Ireland via Anglo-Norman England. The first sheela ... appeared in Ireland during the 1160s, with the earliest wave of Romanesque architectural influence, on the nun's church at Cluain Moccu Nóis. From Cluain, they spread across Ireland ...'[66] Although Bitel does not juxtapose Derbforgaill with the Clonmacnoise sheela-na-gig – indeed, Derbforgaill is curiously absent from *Land of women* – the discursive correspondence is difficult to ignore: a destructive female of unruly passions, either opening Ireland to, or entering Ireland through, Norman influence – which then sweeps across the landscape.

62 Catherine E. Karkov, 'Sheela-na-gigs and other unruly women: images of land and gender in medieval Ireland' in Colum Hourihane (ed.), *From Ireland coming* (Princeton: Index of Christian Art, 2001), pp 313–32 at 325. **63** Karkov, 'Sheela-na-gigs and other unruly women', p. 325. Windele's drawing is reproduced by Karkov as her fig. 12 on p. 326. **64** Ibid., p. 327 and Kelly, *Sheela-na-gigs*, p. 14. **65** Jørgen Anderson, *The witch on the wall: medieval erotic sculpture in the British Isles* (Copenhagen: Rosenkilde and Bagger, 1977), pp 37–9. Cf. Etienne Rynne, 'A pagan Celtic background for sheela-na-gigs?' in Etienne Rynne (ed.), *Figures from the past: studies on figurative art in Christian Ireland in honour of Helen M. Roe* (Dun Laoghaire: Glendale, 1987), pp 189–202. **66** Lisa Bitel, *Land of women: tales of sex and gender from early Ireland* (Ithaca: Cornell University Press, 1996),

4. Acrobatic figure on the chancel arch of the Nuns' Church. Photo: M. Williams

There are, of course, gaps here, no less problematic than the gaps between patronage, abduction and invasion discussed above. Derbforgaill and sheela-na-gigs are never directly equated, but they are in some ways *aligned* and resonant. Each is associated, through the Nuns' Church, with an invasion, whether of the Normans or of *normanitas*. And although the figure on the chancel arch does not share with other sheela-na-gigs the distortions of breasts and genitalia – indeed, the identification of this figure as a sheela is itself problematic[67] – the bodies of both sheelas and Derbforgaill have been contorted, opened up and out for scrutiny and probed as a source of contamination. Their liminal, leaky and violable bodies encode the death of Irish-Ireland and the birth of the Norman. Their seemingly shared threat keeps them in proximity to each other – a proximity that is dangerous because it allows an artistic style or motif to function within a colonial, modernist binary of native/foreign.

The introduction of the Romanesque style into Ireland – even without sheela-na-gigs – is fraught in art historical narratives with this tension between 'native' and 'foreign'. For Françoise Henry, for example, 'the

p. 229. **67** It is more appropriately termed an 'exhibitionist' or 'acrobat' figure; see for example Anthony Weir and James Jerman, *Images of lust: sexual carvings on medieval churches* (London: Batsford, 1986), as well as Karkov, 'Sheela-na-gigs and other unruly women', pp 314–15, and Kelly, *Sheela-na-gigs*, pp 11–13.

Norman invasion marks in Ireland the end of a world, and certainly the death of original artistic endeavor. For centuries after that, art in Ireland was almost completely dominated by foreign models, and the old fire of invention was nearly always lacking'.[68] This appraisal of Irish art after 1169 as distanced both from native 'Irishness' and from originality did not, of course, begin with Henry; in many ways it drove the Celtic Revival of the nineteenth and early twentieth centuries, allowing an overly aestheticized appreciation for the 'Celtic genius' of both pre-Christian and early medieval Ireland.[69] Medieval Irish art was displayed, for example, at World's Fairs, industrial exhibitions and in the newly established National Museum of Ireland side-by-side with (apparently) purely Celtic antiquities, suggesting that early Irish craftsmen had cultivated a distinct visual tradition: colorful, linear, abstract and, most importantly, *native*. The interlaced bands, zoomorphic details and insular scripts of the Book of Kells and the Ardagh Chalice, for example, seemed unaffected by the influence of the classical, Mediterranean figural tradition. Irish culture of the eighth, ninth and tenth centuries was considered by Irish antiquarians and intellectuals to represent a 'Golden Age' before the English domination of the island.[70] The styles and motifs of the eleventh and twelfth centuries – especially, but not only, those carrying Anglo-Norman influence – became foreign 'others', contaminating the purity of native tradition. In his assessment of the historiography of Romanesque architecture, for example, O'Keeffe notes that scholars tend to differentiate between 'Irish Romanesque' and 'Romanesque in Ireland' – the former seeming to denote a more 'local' version of an international style, the latter suggesting importation and dominance.[71] Neither term, O'Keeffe argues, is either useful or accurate: *all* Romanesque architecture is hybrid, at once part of international currents and always-already embedded in local traditions. The distinction perpetuates an essentialist equation between style and nationality.

To be fair, however, Henry's Romanesque Ireland is not the unadulterated, romantic fancy of the Revival. She was, after all, a formalist, trained by Foçillon in the history of style, and she is concerned to situate Irish medieval art in its European context by suggesting continental models and sources, especially for 'the composition of portals [and] part[s] of their decoration.'[72] These continental models, however, are specifically French – following A.K. Porter's pioneering studies of the transmission of sculptural

68 Henry, *Irish art of the Romanesque period*, p. 25. **69** See Karen Eileen Overbey, '(Art)History underground', *Foilsiú* 4:1 (2004), 147–63. **70** T.J. Edelstein (ed.), *Imagining an Irish past: the Celtic Revival, 1840–1940* (Chicago: David and Alfred Smart Museum of Art, University of Chicago, 1992), p. xiv. **71** O'Keeffe, *Romanesque Ireland*, pp 27–33. **72** Henry, *Irish art of the Romanesque period*, p. 205. Of course, Henry's great innovation in terms of stylistic history is the clear and sustained argument for Scandinavian influence in Irish art.

motifs along the medieval pilgrimage routes through France and northern Spain in the eleventh and twelfth centuries,[73] Henry cogently argues for interchange between Irish sculptors and the French Romanesque. In the case of Clonmacnoise, for example, she links the biting horse heads of the Nun's Church's roll mouldings (fig. 3) to similar voussoirs in the churches of the Santoinge, and posits the transmission through Insular artists accompanying Irish kings on continental religious pilgrimage.[74] Here Henry not only affirms the international character of Clonmacnoise's architecture, but also theorizes the role of royal patrons in Ireland's cosmopolitan outlook. In one sense, Henry's work redresses the native/foreign opposition. But throughout the book, she overemphasizes French sources and all but excludes English influence, even characterizing English motifs as 'dry' and 'grim' where Irish forms are 'good-humoured' and 'exhuberant'.[75]

And yet, the Nuns' Church might provide us with a solid example of the hybridity of the Romanesque, of the semiotics of architectural form, and of the extent of the cultural 'knowledge network' in twelfth-century Ireland. It might, if its patron were not so troubling. Certainly, as Ní Ghrádaigh has demonstrated, ambivalence about female patronage has marginalized the Nuns' Church in architectural scholarship. But there is also an anxiety in that scholarship, informed not only by constructions of gender but also by constructions of the colonial: juxtaposed with a narrative of invasion, the Nuns' Church marks the end of the Gaelic and the beginning of Norman Ireland. This anxiety associates the Nuns' Church with nostalgia, and so removes it from that modernist, linear narrative of power, progress and patronage. Ahistoricized, Derbforgaill is a figure of guilt and loss – and with this mythology substituting for a provenance, the Nuns' Church simply cannot be a site where the international and the local interpenetrate.

73 A. Kingsley Porter, *Romanesque sculpture of the pilgrimage roads* (Boston: Marshall Jones Company, 1923). **74** Henry, *Irish art of the Romanesque period*, p. 159. This is a comparison she first published in 1958; see Françoise Henry and George Zarnecki, 'Romanesque arches decorated with human and animal heads', *Journal of the British Archaeological Association*, 3rd ser. 20–1 (1957–8), 1–34. **75** Henry, *Irish art of the Romanesque period*, p. 160.

Names and Naming Conventions Concerning Celtic Peoples in Some Early Ancient Greek Authors[1]

TIMOTHY P. BRIDGMAN

Hecataeus of Miletus in Asia Minor is the first author, whose works have come down to us, to mention 'the land of the Celts'. He was an Ionian ethnographer and mythographer who was writing during the sixth century.[2] Hecataeus was reputed to have traveled widely in Asia and Europe. He may also have recorded descriptions of his trips. Hecateaus wrote a *Periegesis* or guide to world geography that described a coastal voyage around the Mediterranean and the Black Sea. Only about three hundred fragments of his work remain. These are mostly brief quotations in Stephanus of Byzantium's *Ethnika*, which dates from the early sixth century CE. In the *Europa* section of his *Periegesis*, Hecataeus mentions the land of the Celts and their towns. He wrote that Narbon was a trading centre and a *polis* of the Celts.[3] Hecateus calls the inhabitants of Narbon *Narbaioi*. What is interesting in this fragment is that Hecataeus mentions the Celts as the name of a people, making a clear distinction between the larger ethnic name Celts and the smaller subset of Celts who inhabited Narbon, the *Narbaioi*. Thus, from the earliest reference that has come down to us, Hecataeus makes a clear distinction between Celts and *Narbaioi*. He also clearly tells his readers that the inhabitants of Narbon were Celts, but were also referred to by another name. Not only does he make it clear that *Narbaioi* is not the name of a Celtic people, but he also writes that Narbon was a trading centre and city of the Celts. Thus, according to Hecataeus, Narbon was an extremely well-developed Celtic settlement that was big enough for him to refer to it as a

1 The present author would like to thank Professor Joseph Eska who has helped immeasurably in the analysis of many of the names of Celtic peoples mentioned. The opinions expressed in the following, however, are the author's alone. **2** All dates are BCE unless otherwise specified. **3** F. Jacoby, *Die Fragmente der griechischen Historiker* (Berlin: Weidmann, 1923), No. 1 F54; henceforth = *FGrH*.

CSANA Yearbook 7: Four Courts Press, Dublin; ISSN 1649-0096; ISBN 978-1-84682-099-1

polis. Hecataeus also wrote that Nyrax, the location of which is unknown, was also a city of the Celts.[4] Moreover, what is also interesting is that he used the expression *hei keltikei* to mean 'the country of the Celts'.[5] Thus, Hecataeus wrote that the Celts were a people who had two cities on the coast of what is now modern-day southern France and that they had their own lands.

Herodotus of Halicarnassus, on the western coast of what is now Turkey, compiled his *Histories*, sometimes called his *Researches*, about 425. The purpose of his work was to study the events which led up to the war between ancient Greece and the ancient Persians, but he mentions other peoples and phenomena as background. Herodotus gave the geographical term *ek Kelton* 'in/from/out of the land of the Celts'[6] and the name of a city called *Pyrene* that is also mentioned in Avienus.[7] Scholars have assumed that because this name bears a close resemblance to that of the Pyrenees Mountains, the city was located close to where the Pyrenees meet the Mediterranean Sea, but this does not have to be the case. It is rather clear, however, that Herodotus is referring to the west, as he writes that the Ister (Danube) flows through all of Europe and empties into the Euxine (Black Sea) at Istria, which Milesian colonists inhabit. Herodotus also seems to be communicating an extremely Greek view of the geography of Europe to his readers. It is not at all clear whether the city of Pyrene was a Celtic one or not, but it is clear that Herodotus refers to it using a Greek name. He also uses the ancient Greek name *Ister* instead of the ancient Celtic name *Danuuios* and says that it flows through the middle of Europe. The city name Pyrene may well be an ancient Greek name having to do with fire and mining, and not the Celtic name for a town.[8] Herodotus then states that *hoi Keltoi* 'the Celts', live beyond the Pillars of Herakles (Gibraltar) and border on the *Cynetes* who are the westernmost inhabitants of Europe. He appears to be the first ancient author to use the name *hoi Keltoi* in the nominative plural. If it were not for the usage of this name in conjunction with the name *Cynetes*, which he seems to put on par with the name Celts, we would be in a position to assert that Herodotus was using the name of a people. It is rather unclear, however, whether he is. Furthermore, it is unclear whether the name *Cynetes* is ancient Greek, ancient Celtic, an ancient Greek interpretation of an ancient Celtic name, or a combination of the two. What is clear, however, is that Hecataeus referred to Celts living in what is now the south of France and that Herodotus mentioned Celts as living in what is now the Luso-Hispanic Peninsula, as well as along the Danube. The name

4 Jacoby, *FGrH*, No. 1 F56. 5 Aristotle, *Historia animalium* 8 28 606b4; Strabo 4.1.1 C176–7. 6 2.33. 7 *Ora maritima* 559, 565. 8 Anatole Bailly, *Dictionnaire grec-français* (Paris: Hachette, 1959) p. 1705.

Celts, should, therefore, be an overarching name of a people, but it could also be the name of a smaller social grouping. It is more than essential to note, however, that the *Cynetes* are only mentioned in Avienus, *Ora maritima* 201, 566, and Herodotus. Moreover, Strabo and Pliny mention an area called *Cuneus* in western Spain, but say that it was named for a nearby wedge-shaped promontory.[9] This is, however, questionable, as the name is first mentioned in ancient Greek and not in Latin. Appian, however, refers to a people in southwestern Spain called the *Cunei*.[10] Freeman suggests that this people could in fact be a Celtic one based on the root *cuno-* 'hound', from the Indo-European root **ḱwōn-* common in Celtic onomastics.[11] Even if this were the case, *Keltoi* and *Cynetes* would still be referred to on the same level of recognition. Therefore, *Keltoi* would not be the overarching name of a people. Polybius mentions an interesting geographical name in this regard: he writes that there were hills in Thessaly in Greece called *Cynoscephalae* 'the Dogs' Heads'.[12] Although the latter is not used as the name of a people, it does substantiate that names of the sort were in use during the ancient period.

Aristotle (384–322) uses two terms, one of them new in the history of the evolution of names referring to Celtic peoples, in a fragment of Diogenes Laertius 1.1: he writes that among the Celts and Galatians (*Galatai*), there are a people called 'druids' or 'holy ones'.[13] It is clear that 'druids' is not the name of a people, but of a certain echelon of Celtic society. *Galatai* seems to come from a Celtic word **galos* 'brave warrior/fighter'.[14] Thus, *Galatai* may not be the name of a people at all, but may refer to a perceived trait of character of which certain ancient Celts were proud. Ancient Greeks may have heard this word from ancient Celtic speech and thought that it described the name of a people when, in fact, it described a behaviour of a certain sector of ancient Celtic society. On the other hand, if the Greeks in question knew what the term meant in Celtic, they would have participated in fabricating the name of a people when the ancient Celts may simply have used this term to designate 'those who were fighters/warriors' as opposed to 'those who were farmers' or 'those who were involved in commerce'. Interestingly enough, this name was used to designate both western and eastern Celts.[15]

9 Strabo, *Geography* 3.137; Pliny, *Naturalis historia* 4.116; Lat. *cuneus* 'wedge'. **10** Appian, *Hispanica* 57; Gk *Kouneoi*. **11** Philip Freeman, 'The earliest classical sources on the Celts: a linguistic and historical study' (PhD, Harvard University, 1995), p. 45. **12** 28.22.9.4–5, 28.27.28.1–2. **13** V. Rose (ed.), *Aristoteles fragmenta* (Stuttgart: Bibliotheca Scriptorum Graecorum et Romanorum Teubneriana, 1886 [1966]), pp 43–4. **14** Pierre-Yves Lambert, *La langue gauloise* (Paris: Errance, 1994), p. 34. **15** Aelian, *De natura animalium* 17.19; Appian, *Syriakei* 50, etc.; Cassius Dio 41.36, etc.; Lucian, *Dialogi mortuorum* 12.2; Polybius 2.21, etc.; Plutarch, *Aemilius Paulus* 9; Strabo 3.3 C137; 8.7.3 C385.

Pytheas of Massilia, the modern-day Marseille, is thought to have set sail for points north about 325. Nothing survives of his work, only fragments transmitted by later authors. In these scant fragments that have come down to us, Pytheas makes a clear difference between *Brettanikei* and *Celtica*.[16] He says that Britain is an island which is several days sail from *Celtica*. It is to be noted that Pytheas is using the geographical term *Celtica* for the lands inhabited by Celts on the continent of Europe. Moreover, he never calls the inhabitants of Britain Celts, but if *Brettanikei* is a demonstrably Celtic name, as some linguists maintain,[17] there must at least be a linguistic link between the two populations.[18] Furthermore, Tacitus recognized not only that the British and Irish were similar to each other, but that the British were similar to the continental Celts.[19]

Sopater of Paphos was an author of comic poetry of the late fourth/mid third centuries. His work only survives in fragments quoted by other authors. His longest surviving passage comes from a parody entitled the *Galatai*.[20] It is noteworthy that the parody is called the *Galatai*, yet Sopater refers to them as Celts. Thus, the listener/reader would readily believe that the name Celts would be the overarching name of a people and that *Galatai* would have been a subgroup.

Callimachus, writing during the first half of the third century, refers to the great southward movement of the Celts from the Balkan peninsula:[21]

> Yea and one day hereafter there shall come upon us a common struggle, When the Titans of a later day shall rouse up against the Hellenes Barbarian sword and Celtic war, and from the furthest west rush on like snowflakes and in number as the stars when they flock most thickly in the sky.

Here, Callimachus uses the name Celts to designate populations of western Europe, but, then, almost in the same stroke of his writing instrument, uses *Galatai*, making no distinction between the two.[22]

Ephorus of Cyme in Asia Minor, writing during the end of the fifth and fourth centuries, used the name *Keltoi* consistently when referring to Celts in the west, especially in the area of Gadeira which he says was receiving gold, tin and copper from Celtic rivers, confirming some of Herodotus' previous writings. In the fragments of Ephorus' work that have come down

16 Strabo 1.4.3 C104. **17** Communication from Prof. Joseph Eska, 15 August 2005. **18** Strabo 2.4.1 C104 **19** *Agricola* 11, 24. **20** Athenaeus, *Deipnosophistae* 15.160e; G. Kaibel, *Comicorum Graecorum fragmenta* (Berlin: Weidmann, 1899 [1958]), p. 193 F6. **21** 4.172: translation by A.W. Mair, *Callimachus hymns and epigrams, Lycophron, Aratus* (Cambridge: Harvard University Press, 1989), p. 99. **22** 4.184. See Philip Freeman, *The Galatian language: a comprehensive survey of the language of the ancient Celts in Greco-Roman Asia Minor* (Lewiston: Edwin Mellen Press, 2001), pp 5–7.

to us, *Keltoi* or *Keltikei* are used eleven times.[23] *Galatai* is used twice while referring to Celts living in the east, especially in the region of Troy. This situation seems to indicate that a polarization had already taken place, but we cannot at all be sure, because of the fragmentary nature of our evidence, that Ephorus did not use other names, as older authors had done before him. He was, after all, writing only about fifty years after Herodotus. One thing that we can be sure of, however, is that Ephorus did consider the Celts as a major people of the ancient world.[24]

Timaeus of Tauromenium in Sicily was born about 350 and died about 260. He is hailed as the first truly western Greek historian. Timaeus was exiled to Athens, though, when he was about forty-five years old, where he stayed for fifty years. He seems to have written quite a bit about the geography of Celtic rivers, saying that they rush through the Celtic mountains into the Atlantic thrusting forward the water by their flow, drawing it back when they subside.[25] Timaeus seems to have believed that Celtic rivers had tides. He probably dealt more extensively with the area of what is now southern France, perhaps using material from previous authors, such as Hecataeus of Miletus, but there is no trace of any of this, only Strabo's remark that Polybius had found fault with Timaeus because the latter had written that the Rhone river had five mouths.[26] Polybius also complains that Timaeus was wrong concerning the course of the Po.[27] This may indicate that Polybius found Timaeus' description of the water level in the delta quite disconcerting.[28] Polybius also says that Timaeus was ignorant of the topography of Celtic lands. Lionel Pearson feels strongly that Timaeus wrote a detailed account of the Celtic invasion of 390 and the capture of Rome, but we have no idea of the terminology he used.[29] Justin writes that when Dionysius I, tyrant of Syracuse, was in Italy, he was approached by a delegation of Celts after the burning of Rome and that a pact with some of the Celts was reached.[30] Pearson suggests that this information may also have come from Timaeus, but in a previous paper on this subject, I have suggested that Dionysius I, in fact, employed Celts to sack Rome in 390.[31] Therefore, the information may also have come from Philistus. According to Pearson, Timaeus derived the Greek name of Galatia from Galatas, a son of the

23 Jacoby, *FGrH*, IIA, No. 70 F30a, F30b, F30c, F129b, F131a, F131b, F132. **24** Jacoby, *FGrH*, IIA, No. 70 F30b. **25** Jacoby, *FGrH*, Timaeus F73 = Aetius, *Plac.* III.17.6, p. 383 Diels; T.S. Brown, *Timaeus of Tauromenium* (Berkeley: University of California Press, 1958), p. 27. **26** Jacoby, *FGrH*, Timaeus F70 = Strabo 4.1.8. **27** 2.16.13–15 = Jacoby, *FGrH*, Timaeus F68. **28** Lionel Pearson, *The Greek historians of the west. Timaeus and his predecessors* (Atlanta: Scholars Press, 1987), p. 84. **29** Diodorus of Sicily 113.1; Pearson, *Greek Historians* pp 187, 265. **30** 20.5.4. **31** Timothy P. Bridgman, 'The Gallic disaster: was Dionysius I of Syracuse responsible?', presented at the Celtic Studies Association of North America meeting, Virginia Polytechnic Institute & State University, Blacksburg, Virginia, 2001.

Cyclops Polyphemus and the nymph Galatea.[32] In all probability, this information also came from Philistus, because when Dionyius I made a pact with Celts so that they would be seen as allies and not just as mercenaries, he was accused of being a 'barbarian lover'. In order to counteract the negative opinion of Dionysius I, Philistus invented this genealogy about the origin of the *Galatai*. We can be reasonably sure, therefore, that if Timaeus was using this story, he was using the name *Galatai*.

Duris of Samos was a contemporary of Timaeus. Only one fragment of Duris' writings mentions the Celts. Diodorus of Sicily points out that Timaeus' work entitled the *Hellenica* started in 370 and goes on to state that the Romans slew a hundred thousand of the Etruscans, the Galatai and the Samnites during the battle of Sentium in 295.[33] He seems to have used the term *Galatai*.

Polybius was an ancient Greek political leader and historian who was born *c.*200 and who died *c.*118, reputedly of a fall from a horse at the age of 82.[34] His death is highly symbolic of his extremely active life, during which he traveled widely and learned many things. Polybius was the son of Lycortas of Megalopolis in southwestern Arcadia. The latter was a political leader in the Achaean Confederacy during the 180s. Lycortas worked closely with Philopoemen in a failed attempt to deal with Rome on an equal basis. Polybius was responsible for Philopoemen's ashes, which were lain to rest *c.*182. In 180, he was appointed as an envoy to Alexandria and, in 170/169, served as Hipparch of the Confederation. Thus, during most of the first part of his life, Polybius was involved in resisting Rome's take-over of his homeland. When Rome was victorious over Perseus of Macedon at Pydna, however, Callicrates, the arch-opponent of Lycortas and Polybius, and a loyal supporter of Rome, denounced Polybius as not being friendly enough to the Roman people. Callicrates also provided the Romans with a list of one thousand prominent Achaeans who were deported to Italy and detained without trial. Among these one thousand Greeks was Polybius, who was approximately 32 years old. Far from lamenting his plight and becoming hopelessly depressed, Polybius became friend and mentor to P. Cornelius Scipio Aemilianus. Furthermore, he was allowed to remain in Rome during his captivity and became part of the golden circle of power. Polybius may have accompanied Scipio to Spain in 151, to Africa, and may have come back by Hannibal's way over the Alps into Italy. Moreover, he was with Scipio while Carthage was being destroyed in 146. Polybius also went on a trip to the Atlantic. Furthermore, he aided the Romans in their settlement

32 Pearson, *Greek historians*, pp 72–3. **33** Jacoby, *FGrH*, No. 76 F56a = Polybius 2.9.6. **34** Peter S. Derow, 'Polybius' in Simon Hornblower and Anthony Spawforth, *The Oxford classical dictionary* (3rd ed. Oxford: Oxford University Press, 1996), pp 1209–11.

of Greece after the sack of Corinth *c.*146, and visited Alexandria, Sardis and perhaps Numantia in 133.

In addition to having an extremely active and varied life, Polybius was an intellectual and a historian who became utterly fascinated by Rome and how it was possible that it could have conquered and taken over virtually the whole of the known world in *c.*53 years. Polybius wrote a work called the *Histories* in forty books of which a substantial amount survives in both the original text and fragments. In this work, he also endeavoured to show how the Romans ruled, how other peoples of the ancient world reacted to Roman rule and the effect that this process had on all sides. In order for Roman political and military power to control the known world, it had to knock out the power of other major players in the ancient world, such as the ancient Greeks, Etruscans, Carthaginians and, of course, the Celts.

Polybius uses the name *Keltoi* 131 times. Within that name, however, there is one notable variation which is *Italian Keltous*.[35] He used this twice, seemingly recognizing that there were Celts in Italy and that this fact was worth mentioning. Polybius uses the name *Galatai* 120 times. Within this name, Polybius uses several variations: one is *tōn Alpeōn Galatas*, seeming to consider that these individuals needed to be recognized as separate from other *Galatai*.[36] These two names, however, may simply have been based on geographical notions of ethnography. Polybius uses the ethnonym *hoi Boioi kaloumenoi Galatai* 'Boii who have been called Galatai' once.[37] This may suggest that *Galatai* is not an ethnonym, but refers to a trait or activity, viz., being good fighters/warriors. Polybius may also have been identifying *Boii* as *Galatai* here. Our author also used the ethnonym *Allobrigōn kaloumenōn Galatōn* 'the Allobroges who have been called Galatai', perhaps suggesting that the *Allobroges* were a smaller group included in the *Galatai* or that the *Allobroges* were also great fighters/warriors. Polybius uses the name *Ardues Keltoi*, but only once.[38] He may have been identifying the *Ardues* as Celts. Once again, Polybius felt that he needed to reinforce the name *Ardues* with *Keltoi*, perhaps to emphasize in his own mind that the *Ardues* were, indeed, Celts. Polybius may have felt that it was doubtful or questionable that the *Ardues* were *Keltoi*. The name *Ardues* does appear to be Celtic, perhaps based on the root *ard-* 'high'.[39] Thus, this name may mean something like 'the high ones', but it could also have meant something along the lines of 'those who worship the goddess Arduuna/Arduona'. It seems unlikely in this case that this would be the name of a people, but would rather refer to a religious activity. Polybius also uses the double ethnonyms *Galatai Rhigosages* once and *Aegosagae Galatai* twice in Book 5, perhaps seeking to specify that the

35 1.3.4, 1.6.6. **36** 2.21.4. **37** 3.40.6. **38** 3.47.3.2. **39** Xavier Delamarre, *Dictionnaire de la langue gauloise* (Paris: Errance, 2001), p. 45; Lambert, *Langue gauloise*, p. 76.

Rhigosagae and the *Aegosagae* were, in fact, good fighters/warriors.[40] *Rhigosagae* seems to be a Celtic name which may mean 'those who look for/search out the king'.[41] In my opinion, it would be difficult to accept this as the name of a Celtic people. *Aegosagae* < *Aidosages*/*Aigosages* < **Aidisages* or **Aidusages* is also a Celtic name which may mean something like 'those who search for fire/valour'.[42] Polybius also uses the ethnonym *Thrakei Galatōn* once in Book 8.[43] This seems to be simply a geographical description of a location to which some Celtic fighters had moved. Polybius uses the double ethnonym *Tolistobogiois Galatais* once in Book 21.[44] The latter once again appears to be a way of identifying the *Tolistobogiois* as good fighters/warriors, perhaps suggesting that if *Galatai* were an ethnonym, then those individuals who made up the *Tolistobogiois* would be a subgroup of the larger group called *Galatai*. Polybius uses the name *Asian Galatōn* three times in Books 21, 29 and 30.[45] This name seems once again to be built on a geographical description. It seems clear that Polybius uses double ethnonyms in part to establish a geographical location, but also to either identify one group as a subset of another or to identify that a particular group was known for being fierce fighters. This leads one to ask the question whether Polybius knew what *Galatai* meant in Continental Celtic. Although from what we know of his life, it does not seem that he had any fluency in Continental Celtic, he did travel widely and perhaps had repeated contact with Celtic-speaking peoples.[46] The question then becomes: in what language did they communicate? The obvious answer would be ancient Greek, as it is well known that many ancient Celts did in fact speak Greek, especially for commercial purposes. Also, the *polis* of Massalia was at first at least a bilingual city, Celtic and Greek, and, then, a trilingual city, Celtic, Greek and Latin.[47] What is known to a far lesser degree is how many Celts spoke and/or read and wrote ancient Greek during Polybius' lifetime. He may also have employed translators.

In Book 2, Polybius mentions a completely new name, *Anares*, three times.[48] The *Anares*, according to Polybius, seem to have lived near Massalia and on the other bank of the Po by the Appenines. This does not appear to be a Celtic name and where it comes from is uncertain.[49] Polybius also

40 5.53.3.3, 5.77.2.3, 5.78.6.1–2. **41** Communication from Prof. Joseph Eska, 14 December 2005. **42** Ibid. **43** 8.22.1.1. **44** 21.37.2.4. **45** 21.38.2.1 = Plutarch, *The virtuous deeds of women* 22, 29.22.4.6, 30.28.1.1. **46** On bilingualism in the ancient world, see J.N. Adams, *Bilingualism and the Latin language* (Cambridge: Cambridge University Press, 2003), pp 184–99 and 687–724; J.N. Adams, Mark Janse and Simon Swain (eds), *Bilingualism in ancient society* (Oxford: Oxford University Press, 2002), pp 11–12, 29–30, 419–29. **47** Polybius 3.41; Caesar, *B. Civil.* 34.4; Strabo 4.1.5; Livy 38.17.11; Justin 43.4.1; Varro apud Isidore of Seville, *Etym.* 15.1.63; Saint Jerome, *In Galat.* 2.426, p. 543 Migne. See also A. Momigliano, *Alien wisdom:. the limits of Hellenization* (Cambridge: Cambridge University Press, 1990), p. 55, and Adams, *Bilingualism*, p. 191. **48** 2.17.7, 32.2, 34.5. **49** Communication from Prof. Joseph Eska, 28 October 2006.

mentions another new name, *Agones*, but only once.[50] This does not seem to be a Celtic name either, but may be related to the ancient Greek word for 'struggle'.[51] Another new name mentioned in Book 2 is *Boii*. He mentions this name twenty times. *Boios* is attested as a personal name and appears to have meant something like 'fighter/warrior'.[52] Thus, once again, it does not appear to be the name of a people, but the name seems to describe the same general idea as *Galatai*. In Book 2, Polybius introduces another new name, *Cenomani*, which appears in ancient Greek as *Gonomanoi*.[53] This name is mentioned four times and could be Celtic meaning something like 'of good birth'.[54] This could constitute the name of a people, but it sounds more like a name that corresponds to an echelon of society rather like the *Aristoi* in ancient Greek. Polybius also mentions the *Gaesatae* four times. This translates as 'spearthrowers'.[55] As every Celtic army comprised spearthrowers, this cannot be considered the name of a people. Within this name, there is a variation that occurs twice: the *Gaisatai Galatai* 'Galatian Gaesatae'.[56] These individuals appear to have lived on the Rhone to the south of the Alps. The name would translate as 'spearthrowing warriors' and it is uncertain as to why Polybius found it necessary to use such a reinforced name, but one may suggest that he was again identifying a special group of individuals as both spearthrowers and warriors. Thus, it seems doubtful that *Gaisatai Galatai* could be the name of a Celtic people. Polybius also introduces the name *Insubres*, written *Insombres* in ancient Greek, for the first time in Book 2. He uses it sixteen times. Once again, not only does this not seem to be recognizably Celtic, but it is extremely obscure.[57] Polybius also uses the name *Laevi*, written *Laoi* in ancient Greek, but only once.[58] This does not appear to be Celtic,[59] but it seems to translate from ancient Greek as something to do with 'people'. Polybius also introduces the new name *Lebecii*, written *Lebekioi* in ancient Greek, in Book 2, but only uses it once.[60] It, once again, does not appear to be Celtic.[61] Polybius introduces another new name in Book 2, the

50 2.15.8. **51** Communication from Prof. Joseph Eska, 28 October 2006. **52** Alfred Bammesberger, 'Celtic Boios' in D.Q. Adams (ed.), *Festschrift for Eric P. Hamp* (Washington, DC: Institute for the Study of Man, 1997), vol. 1, pp 60–6; Delamarre, *Dictionnaire*, p. 70. **53** 2.17.4, 2.23.2–3, 2.24.7–8, 2.32.2.4. **54** Communication from Prof. Joseph Eska, 9 November 2005, but see P. De Bernardo Stempel, 'Ptolemy's Celtic Italy and Ireland: a lingustic analysis' in David N. Parsons and Patrick Sims-Williams (eds), *Ptolemy: towards a linguistic atlas of the earliest Celtic place-names of Europe* (Aberystwyth: CMCS Publications, 2000), p. 91, who feels that Ptolemy's *Cenomanōn* would mean 'the far going ones'. She makes no mention of Polybius' *Gonomanoi*. Patrick Sims-Williams, *Ancient Celtic place-names in Europe and Asia Minor* (Oxford: Blackwell Publishing Ltd., 2006), p. 256, remains circumspect, but does not mention *Gonomanoi* either. **55** 2.22.1–2, 2.28.3, 2.28.7, 2.30.5; Nonius 555; Servius, *Ad Aen.* 8.660; Delamarre, *Dictionnaire*, pp 146–7; Lambert, *Langue gauloise*, p. 202. **56** 2.23.1, 34.2–3. **57** Communications from Prof. Joseph Eska, 8 January 2006 and 18 July 2007. **58** 2.16.4. **59** Communication from Prof. Joseph Eska, 28 October 2006. **60** 2.17.4. **61** Communication from Prof. Joseph Eska, 28 October 2006.

Senones.[62] This name does seem to be linguistically Celtic and would translate roughly as 'the old divine ones' or 'the sages'. Even though the *Senones* are described here as a distinct people on the Adriatic coast, this, once again, does not seem to be the name of a Celtic people, but rather a name that would correspond to an echelon of a society, perhaps the druids. Polybius introduces another new name in Book 2, the *Lingones*, which contains the Celtic root 'jump' and the suffix *-on-* meaning 'divine'.[63] Thus, it could translate roughly as 'the divine jumpers'. This, once again, does not strike the present author as the name of a people, but may perhaps relate to a type of ritual or religious activity. Curiously, our author also uses another name from ancient Greek, *hoi Transalpinoi*, that translates as 'the Transalpine ones'.[64] This is clearly not the name of a people, but is based on a geographical factor. Polybius also uses the name *tōn Transalpinōn* 'Transalpine Celts'.[65] Our author also introduces the name *Taurisci* which is clearly based on the ancient Greek *tauros* 'bull'.[66] Granted that this could be a translation of a Celtic name into ancient Greek, this possibility does not seem to fit the pattern that we have seen in Polybius. In the fragments of Polybius' Book 34, the ethnonym *tois Tauriskois tois Norikois* 'Noric Taurisci' is used, but only once.[67] This name seems to be based on a geographical factor and is clearly not the name of a Celtic people. He also uses the name *Veneti* and considers it the name of a Celtic people.[68] Justin's account of the *Vestigia Graeci moris* in Italy includes Perusia, Spina and Adria as ancient Greek cities, in addition to those noted in other sources. Among the Hellenic migrants, Justin mentions the *Veneti*, who came from Troy after its capture, led by Antenor.[69] Virgil knew this story.[70] Pliny also cites Cato's authority on this story.[71] Strabo, however, knew that the opinion concerning the *Veneti* was divided, some saying that they were Celts, but others writing that some *Eneti* from Paphlagonia joined Antenor and went there.[72] Years before, Herodotus had written that the *Eneti* were not Celts, but dressed like Celts and spoke a different language.[73] The name *Veneti* does seem to be Celtic, but they were first referred to in Herodotus as *Eneti*, which does not seem to be Celtic, so there is some confusion.[74] Polybius also uses the name *Veneti*, but only once.[75]

Polybius also introduces the ethnonym *Allobrogon*, often transcribed as *Allobroges*, in Book 3, where he uses it four times.[76] This name does analyze linguistically as Celtic having the sense of 'those who are from another land'

62 2.17.7, 2.20.1, 2.21.7. Delamarre, *Dictionnaire*, p. 229; Lambert, *Langue gauloise*, p. 34. **63** 2.17.7. Communication from Prof. Joseph Eska, 12 November 2005. **64** 2.15.8, 2.19.1. **65** 2.21.5. **66** 2.15.8, 2.28.3, 2.30.6, 34.10.14.1 = Strabo 5.6.12 C208. Communication from Prof. Joseph Eska, 14 December 2005. **67** 34.10.3 = Strabo 5.6.12 C208. **68** 2.17.5–6. **69** 20.1.6.12. **70** 1.1.1–2. **71** *Naturalis historia* 3.130. **72** 5.1.4. Pearson, *Greek historians*, pp 82–3. **73** 1.196. **74** On the different peoples labeled as *Veneti*, see J. Loicq, 'Sur les peuples au nom Venète ou assimilé dans l'occident européen', *Etudes Celtiques* 35 (2003), 133–65. **75** 2.17.5. **76** 3.50.1, 3.50.3, 3.51.7.2,

or 'the foreigners'.[77] Our author also uses the expression *kaloumenoi Galatai* 'the Allobroges who have been called Galatai', as if the *Allobrogon* were a smaller social grouping within the *Galatai* or as if they were simply being identified as great fighters/warriors. Polybius also introduces the geographical name *ton Brettanikou neson*, the British Isles, already known from a previous author, perhaps Pytheas of Massalia, but only once, in Book 3.[78] He also uses the geographical term *Brettanikeis*.[79] In Book 3, he also introduces the ethnonym *Taurini*. It appears once in Book 3 and once in the fragments of Polybius' Book 34. This does not seem to be Celtic, but rather is based on Latin *taurus* 'bull'.[80] Once again, it could well be a translation of a Celtic name in which case, it would have meant 'the bulls'. This does not seem, however, to fit the pattern of analysis that we have studied in Polybius' work. In Book 15, Polybius introduces the ethnonym *Bastarnes*, but is far from certain himself that these individuals were Celts.[81] This would be supported by the fact that their name does not seem to analyze as Celtic.[82] In Book 21, the ethnonym *Tectosages* appears, but only once.[83] This appears to be linguistically Celtic, meaning 'possession seekers' and a possible name of a Celtic people.[84] It also seems, however, to confirm an ancient Greek and Roman stereotype of the Celts as marauders, thieves, raiders, those who pillage. As we cannot evaluate whether Polybius knew or could at least understand Continental Celtic, we must assume that he did not invent this name in Celtic using a Greek/Roman stereotype. He may, however, have used translators. We may conclude, however, that this name may have been used for mercenaries, as these individuals sought gain through military service in foreign armies. In Book 31, the ethnonym *Kammanous/Cammani* is introduced, but is only used once.[85] This appears to be a Celtic ethnonym, meaning 'those who walk/march or the walkers/marchers'.[86] It could also simply be a military term instead of the name of a Celtic people.

The ethnonym *Trocmi* appears in the fragments of Polybius' Book 31, but only once.[87] This name is possibly of Celtic origin.[88] The ethnonym *Oxybii* appears six times in Polybius' Book 33.[89] It is not a Celtic name, but rather is built on the ancient Greek *oxy-* 'sharp'.[90] Also in Polybius' Book 33, the ethnonym *Decietae* appears and is used three times.[91] This is, in all probability,

3.51.9.2. **77** Delamarre, *Dictionnaire*, p. 34; Lambert, *Langue gauloise*, pp 36, 59, 61. **78** 3.57.3. **79** 34.10.7.3–4 = Strabo 4.2.1 C190. **80** Delamarre, *Dictionnaire*, p. 246; Lambert, *Langue gauloise*, p. 124. **81** 15.6.2.1. **82** Communication from Prof. Joseph Eska, 15 December 2005. **83** 21.39.2.2. **84** Communication from Prof. Joseph Eska, 1 December 2005. **85** 31.1.1. **86** Delamarre, *Dictionnaire*, p. 85; Lambert, *Langue gauloise*, p. 192. **87** 31.8.2.2. **88** See Sims-Williams, *Ancient place-names*, p. 275, who says that *Trocmi* has been regarded as Celtic, but that there seems to be no general agreement as to etymology or meaning. **89** 33.9.2.2, 33.9.8.4, 33.10.2.1, 33.10.5.1, 33.10.9.2, 33.11.1.2. **90** Communication from Prof. Joseph Eska, 12 April 2006. **91** 33.9.8.5, 33.10.5.4, 33.10.9.1.

a Celtic name based on the root *dek-* and would mean 'ten'.[92] Thus, this ethnonym may mean 'the ten' and could well be a military designation. In the fragments of Book 34 of Polybius' work, the ethnonym *Pictones* appears once.[93] This is not a Celtic name because it is based on the Latin 'those who have been painted' and not on Celtic.[94] Moreover, body painting was an extremely widespread activity in the Celtic world. The ethnonym *Namnitae* appears in the fragments of Polybius' Book 34, but only once[95]. It could well be a Celtic name meaning 'the ninth ones' and, consequently, may be compared to *Decietae*, the two being used as military labels, possibly of units or groups.[96] It could also, however, mean 'the ninth valley, stream, river'.[97] In the fragments of Polybius' Book 34, the ethnonym *Salassi* also occurs, but only once.[98] This does not appear to be Celtic, but may be built on the Latin *sal-* 'salt'. Also in the fragments of Polybius' Book 34, the ethnonym *Morinorum Britannicum* appears, but only once.[99] The name *Morini* appears to be Celtic and clearly has something to do with the sea, living near the sea or being a sailor.[100] *Britannicum* serves simply as a geographical identifier, letting the reader know that Polybius was referring to the *Morini* in Britain as opposed to those who lived on the continent. It could be the name of a Celtic people, but could also have been a general name referring to a sector of Celtic society or even more generally, to people living on the coast as opposed to those living inland. In the fragments of Polybius' Book 35, the ethnonym *Belli* is used twice.[101] This does seem to be a Celtic name, meaning 'those who are strong, forceful'.[102] It may indeed be the name of a Celtic people, but, on the other hand, may simply be yet another term describing the prowess in battle of a certain sector of Celtic society. In the fragments of Polybius' Book 35, another new ethnonym appears, *Titti*.[103] This could be Celtic, but there is no agreement as to etymology or meaning.[104] Finally, the ethnonym *Arauacon/Aravacae* is used seven times in the fragments of Polybius' Book 35.[105] This name could be Celtic if the *-a* in the first part of the name *ara-* was in fact extremely weak and could correspond to *are-*. In this case, the first part of the name *Arauacon/Aravacae* could be translated as 'in front of' or 'close to', but there is little evidence for this development.[106] It could also have the sense of 'temple' or 'cheek', which would also fit better with the second part of the name *–uacon/-vacae*, which could be derived into

92 Communication from Prof. Joseph Eska, 4 November 2005. **93** 34.10.6.1 = Strabo 4.2.1 C190. **94** Communication from Prof. Joseph Eska, 1 April 2006. **95** 34.10.6.1 = Strabo 4.2.1 C190. **96** Lambert, *Langue gauloise*, pp 44, 130, 132. **97** Delamarre, *Dictionnaire*, pp 195–6. **98** 34.10.18.4 = Strabo 4.6.12 C208. **99** 34.15.1.5 = Pliny, *NH* 4.121. **100** Delamarre, *Dictionnaire*, p. 194; Lambert, *Langue gauloise*, p. 34. **101** 35.2.3.2, 35.2.11.2. **102** Delamarre, *Dictionnaire* p. 62. **103** 35.2.3.2, 35.2.11.2. **104** Communication from Prof. Joseph Eska, 18 July 2007. **105** 35.2.4.1–2, 35.2.10.1, 35.2.10.2–3, 35.2.13.1, 35.3.3.1, 35.3.4.2, 35.3.9.4. **106** Delamarre, *Dictionnaire* p. 45; Lambert, *Langue gauloise*, pp 41–7, 190.

something like 'cheek', but there is little evidence for this.[107] In this light, there is a possibility that the name *Arauacon/Aravacae* could have meant something like 'those who have curved temples/cheeks', perhaps in reference to an obvious physical feature of which those who identified themselves as *Arauacon/Aravacae* were proud or one that others imposed on them because they found it unusual or strange.

It is clear that in the fragments that have come down to us of authors writing before Polybius, only two names of Celtic peoples were used consistently and continuously: *Keltoi* and *Galatai*. *Keltoi* is unquestionably the oldest name to have been used by ancient Greek authors. There seems, however, to be no general agreement as to what the ethnonym *Keltoi* denotes. It seems that its root *kel-* is followed by a suffix **-to* or **-tā* used to nominalise verbal roots.[108] The root itself could mean 'hide, conceal, be warm, be cold, freeze, drive, urge, hurry up, rise above, tower above, tower over, rise up, entice, betwitch, beguile, deceive, cheat, swindle, betray, fight'. In this list of possibilities, there are some that just do not make sense given what we know of the Celts: it would be difficult to accept that the root *kel-* meant something like 'those who are warm', 'those who are cold', 'those who freeze', 'those who are frozen', or 'those who drive, urge, hurry up'. On the other hand, 'those who hide, conceal', 'those who rise above', 'those who tower above/over', 'those who entice, bewitch, beguile', 'those who deceive, cheat, swindle, betray' and 'those who hit, beat, punch, strike' seem plausible, but linguists are not yet in a position to choose between them. Taking into account the names discussed in this article, many express the theme of being good fighters/warriors (*Galatai*, *Boii*, *Belli*). It would not be beyond reason to hypothesize that *Keltoi* meant something like 'those who smash, strike, fight'. Other possibilities in the original list point to a theme of strength: 'those who rise above/tower above/tower over'. On the other hand, 'those who hide/conceal', 'those who entice, beguile, bewitch' and 'those who deceive, cheat, swindle, betray' are all still possibilities. If we accept that the ethnonym *Keltoi* meant 'those who smash, strike fight', it would confirm the major stereotype of the ancient Greeks and Romans regarding the Celts. It would also confirm why Celts served as mercenaries all over the ancient world. If the ethnonym *Keltoi*, however, meant 'those who hide/conceal', 'those who cheat/swindle/betray' or 'those who entice/bewitch/beguile', we would have no clues as to which to pick, perhaps with the exception of 'those who entice/bewitch/beguile', which could refer to the practice of druidism. *Keltos/Keltoi* is never attested as an ethnic name in ancient Continental

107 Communication from Prof. Joseph Eska, 18 July 2007. **108** Communication from Prof. Joseph Eska, 25 August 2005.

Celtic.[109] It is, however, attested as a personal name, but its meaning is not known.[110]

Polybius introduces forty-three names in his *Histories* that do not appear in the fragments of previous authors that have come down to us. Where did he get these names? Of the forty-three new names, only fifteen of them, far less than half, analyze as linguistically Celtic. Of these fifteen, at least three names seem to refer to different sectors of Celtic society, such as 'those of good birth', 'the old divine ones', 'the divine jumpers', and, thus, cannot be considered as ethnonyms. In the final analysis, only two ethnonyms can reasonably be considered as names of Celtic peoples: 'those who walk/march', although this may be a military label, and 'those who have curved temples/cheeks', although this is a questionable interpretation of the name *Aravacae*. The vast majority of the rest of the names which analyze as Celtic refer to military exploits or prowess on the battlefield, or to mercenary service (*Tectosages*). One exception, however, is the *Allobroges* 'those who are from another land/foreigners'. This could either be an emic or etic name, but the present writer believes that it has more chance of being an etic name because if a people implants themselves in a foreign land, they will usually still use their emic name. It seems fairly clear that if such a people had adopted a name themselves that it would have comprised the name of a homeland or region. *Allobroges* seems roughly equivalent to the Breton name for the French, *ar C'halloued*, using the pan-Celtic root *gall-* 'foreigner'. Eight names, and, perhaps, a ninth, have a geographical component which simply indicates where the individuals in question were living, such as *hoi Transalpinoi* 'the Transalpine ones' or *tois Tauriskois tois Norikois* 'Noric Taurisci'. These are clearly not the names of Celtic peoples, but geographical locations. Two names seem to refer to religious practices: *Lingones* 'the divine jumpers' and the *Ardues Keltoi* 'the high/elevated Celts'. As such, these cannot be understood as names of Celtic peoples.

Fifteen of the ethnonyms studied above are not Celtic. Many of these appear to be built on ancient Greek and/or Latin roots. The present author fails to comprehend why a Celtic people would choose a name based on ancient Greek or Latin as an emic name. If this were true, some names of ancient Greek and/or Latin tribes would be Celtic and/or Germanic, and this is simply not the case. Finally, there are three names which are of unknown origin.

The question remains: where did Polybius get all these new names? One solution to this question would be that he got them from works of previous authors that have not come down to us. While we are in a position to accept

109 Communication from Prof. Joseph Eska, 26 August 2005. **110** Ibid.

this solution, it would not account for the consistency of the two names *Keltoi* and *Galatai* that appear in every author before Polybius. Another solution consists of hypothesizing that Polybius picked up these names when he was on his travels in the west, especially when he was on campaign with Scipio. Within this solution, we could envisage that he would have got these names from ancient Greek/Latin speakers in places such as Massalia where they came into frequent and repeated contact with Celts. This would entail believing that those ancient Greek/Latin speakers had their own etic names for Celts with whom they came into contact or that they heard these names from other ancient Greek or Latin speakers and then transmitted them to Polybius. A third solution would be that Polybius made up these names out of whole cloth. It is the present author's suggestion that the real answer is a combination of these three solutions. It is also the present writer's contention that each name must be analysed on a case-by-case basis. It appears quite clearly from the research above that we must start to reconsider how ancient Celtic society is presented to the reader of classical texts. It certainly does not seem to have been a society that was divided into many different tribes, each comprising its own name, as has been assumed by generations of classicists, Celticists, historians, archaeologists and linguists.

Index